The Razor Edge of Balance

A study of Virginia Woolf

JANE NOVAK

The Razor Edge of Balance
A study of Virginia Woolf

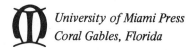

University of Miami Press
Coral Gables, Florida

Copyright © 1975 by University of Miami Press

Designed by Anne Hertz

Manufactured in the United States of America

Library of Congress Cataloging in Publication Data

Novak, Jane, 1917-
    The razor edge of balance.

    Bibliography: p.
    1. Woolf, Virginia Stephen, 1882-1941–Criticism
and interpretation. I. Title.
PR6045.072Z837   823'.9'12   72-85111
ISBN 0-87024-247-4

The photo of the Godrevy Lighthouse on page 66 was taken by Studio St. Ives, Ltd., St. Ives, Cornwall.

for Alice and Charles
and for Tabor

Contents

Illustrations

Preface

Virginia Woolf was supernormally aware of that oscillation between opposites which characterizes the mind's universe. Her diary records the rhythms of elation and melancholy: "so divinely happy one day; so jaded the next." The moments of weariness were not boredom but strain from her own acute sense of doubleness: "how my brain is jaded with the conflict of two types of thought—the critical and the creative; how I am harassed by the strife and jar and uncertainty without." Her metaphors for happiness, "a trout in a stream, a flag in a breeze," are of entities in perfect tension with living forces. But her temperament was responsive to the flux of disturbing alternation; she heard the dialogue between the masculine and the feminine selves within her, felt the shifts between the open sensibility of the brilliant child and the cool analysis of the skeptical adult. Even her wit play was characteristically that of reversal: hyperbole and deflation, sudden self-mockery in the midst of solemnity. She understood her own duality; she sensed that of others.

Her sharp awareness of the contrasts of life naturally extended to large questions. As a literary critic she considered and reconsidered a variety of double terms: fact and vision, art and life, the inner and the outer world, order and chaos, mutability and continuity. In society she saw the value of order and tradition but abhorred their tendency to harden into tyrannical dogmas and institutions; she fought for individual freedom but acknowledged the dangers of withdrawal and solipsism.

Yet her aim as an artist was not only to imitate the warring antagonisms in human life, but to find a fictional form that would hold all opposites in a state of momentary wholeness yielding insight, a tense state that was "not so much unity," Richard Ellmann observes, "as the threat of a breakdown of unity." In *To the Lighthouse* Virginia Woolf embodied in a symbolic action this difficult struggle for harmony, form, and fleeting revelation: Lily Briscoe, an artist, seeks throughout the novel to compose the refractory elements of a painting and to experience a vision by achieving in its design "the razor edge of balance between two opposite forces."

Using this image of a search for balance as a key, I have studied Virginia Woolf's deliberately unsystematized formal theories in relation to the structure of her first five novels, considering Lily's vision as the high point closing the first phase of her career. *To the Lighthouse* was the culmination of her early search to realize the goals that had been clear to her from the first days of her apprenticeship.

My method has obvious drawbacks. The metaphor of a search for a tenuous balance can be applied to the work of any form-conscious artist; it is an elastic concept, inviting equivocation. But that very looseness made it uncommonly useful to Virginia Woolf. For all its imprecision as a critical tool, it was an essential one for her, for it was her metaphor for self, for mind, and for creation. It is the pattern of the plots of her novels and the shaping principle for her speculations on aesthetics and fictional form; it is central to her judgments as a literary critic. The primary architectonic principle of her fiction was the powerful disposal of contrasting elements. She used the images of precarious balancing, the balancer, and balance again and again, exploring their psychological and aesthetic ramifications. In her novels she condemned exercises of power, between persons or by society, which threatened individual equilibrium. In spite of the great body of Woolf criticism, I believe that more exploration of this central image is useful.

Part 1 is an analysis of Virginia Woolf as a speculative theorist, distrusting rules, yet continually considering the variety of "opposite forces" which must be controlled by the novelist. As a critic she made use of the painter's theories of compositional balance for the novel and analyzed the "perspective" by which writers ordered the world of their fictions. Part 2 is a formal analysis of her first five novels in terms of that tentative theory. Wherever it seems relevant to her artistic choices, I have used biographical material with full consciousness of its temptation to error. This is not a critical biography, nor a psychoanalytic study, but an examination of what may be empirically observed as changes in method from novel to novel in relation to her aesthetic speculations.

Others indeed have addressed themselves to similar problems, but many letters and notes here included add new insights. Of particular interest are selections from the voluminous correspondence between the young Virginia Stephen and Violet Dickinson, grandniece of the Victorian letter writer and novelist, Emily Eden. (Miss Dickinson was twelve years older than her young friend; Virginia called her "a mother abbess" and wrote her almost daily in the years before her marriage. Violet saved Virginia's life during her severe collapse and suicide attempt after the death of Virginia's father, Sir Leslie Stephen, Victorian critic, biographer, historian, and philosopher.) In addition, early reviews, unrepublished, are quoted. The unpublished Monks House Papers in the University of Sussex Library also furnish evidence.

The resulting study examines Virginia Woolf's first five novels in relation to a controlling idea characteristic of her temperament, aesthetics, criticism, and fictional theory. I have attempted to shed more light on an already brilliantly illuminated subject; I have necessarily touched on areas considered by others. And because my subject is chiefly the dualities of her fiction and the architectonics that controlled its forms, I have necessarily ignored many other aspects.

The search for primary material has led me to the Berg Collection of the New York Public Library, to the British Museum, to the University of Sussex Library, to King's College Library in Cambridge, and to Lewes in Sussex. Everywhere it has brought me into the company of intelligent, sensitive, warm, and generous people. A Leverhulme Visiting

Fellowship at the University of East Anglia provided me both with these rich opportunities for discovery and with a year of anglophiliac delight, that as a matter of good form, I strove to understate. There is no way, however, to overstate my gratitude for the award. The generosity of Lord Annan of University College, London University, and Professors Harry Allen, Malcolm Bradbury, and Roger Fowler of the School of English and American Studies, UEA, was characteristic of the help I enjoyed at every turn in England.

Particular thanks are due to Professor Quentin Bell of the University of Sussex, the nephew, literary executor, and indispensable biographer of Virginia Woolf, and to Olivier Bell; both their great kindness and their patient correction of my errors are greatly appreciated. I offer long years of gratitude to Professor Clark M. Emery of the University of Miami for his warm interest in the manuscript and for his cool criticism of it. I am grateful to Professor James E. Miller, Jr., of the University of Chicago and to Professor Don Herring of Wabash College for the provocative and probing questions that directed my work in the early stages. Professor Wayne Booth of the University of Chicago was also kind enough to read it and to comment. None of these mentors can be held responsible for my flaws of judgment.

I am happy to thank Dr. Lola L. Szladits, curator of the Berg Collection of the New York Public Library, for leading me to the material most fruitful for my purposes and for her continuing assistance in preparing the manuscript. I thank also Adrian N. Peasgood, Sub-Librarian of the University of Sussex Library, and Dr. A. L. N. Munby, librarian, and Penelope Bullock, archivist of King's College Library, for their help. I am grateful, too, for the critical observations and support of my colleagues at the University of Illinois, Chicago Circle, Professors Nancy Cirillo, Irving Miller, and Elizabeth Wright. The late Ethel O. Comber of Penzance, Cornwall, made a literal voyage to the lighthouse on my behalf on a day of faint blue skies and bright emerald seas; I wish I could thank her again.

My husband, Tabor, has been unendingly helpful, patient, and hopeful that the task would be finished at last. For him, thanks are not enough.

Acknowledgments

I gratefully acknowledge permission from Professor Quentin Bell and the heirs of the Woolf Estate and from the Henry W. and Albert A. Berg Collection, the New York Public Library, Astor, Lenox, and Tilden Foundations, to quote from Virginia Woolf's correspondence, holograph notes, and manuscripts; from the Woolf Estate, the Hogarth Press, and Harcourt Brace Jovanovich, Inc. for permission to quote from her works; from the Woolf Estate for permission to quote from Leonard Woolf's works; from the Berg Collection of the New York Public Library and from George W. Rylands of King's College, Cambridge, literary executor on behalf of the college for the E. M. Forster Estate, to quote from E. M. Forster's letters to Virginia Woolf.

I am grateful for permission from the Cambridge University Press to quote from Roger Fry's *Last Lectures* (1939); from Doubleday & Company to quote from Roger Fry's *Transformations* (1956); from Harcourt Brace Jovanovitch, Inc. for permission to quote from Jean Guiguet's *Virginia Woolf and Her Works,* from Leonard Woolf's *Sowing, Beginning Again, The Journey Not the Arrival Matters,* and *Downhill All the Way,* from E. M. Forster's *Aspects of the Novel* and *A Passage to India;* and from Mrs. Pamela Diamand and the Hogarth Press to quote from Roger Fry's *The Artist and Psychoanalysis* (1924); for permission from Jean Guiguet and the Hogarth Press to quote from Jean Guiguet's *Virginia Woolf and Her Works.* I am grateful also for permission from the Hogarth Press to quote from Forster's *Aspects of the Novel* (1927).

I am grateful to Mrs. Ian Parsons of Lewes, Sussex for her great courtesy in permitting the use of the portrait of Virginia Woolf by Vanessa Bell that is reproduced on page xviii.

I acknowledge permission from Nigel Nicolson and Professor Joanne Trautmann, editors of the Virginia Woolf correspondence, and from the University of Sussex Library to quote from materials in the Monks House Papers. *The Virginia Woolf Newsletter* (Columbia University) has given permission for the use of material that originally appeared as "Virginia Woolf—A Fickle Jacobean."

part One

Problems of balance

Portrait of Virginia Woolf painted by her sister, Vanessa Bell, in 1913.

chapter One

In search of balance

For the thirty-two years during which she wrote eight novels,
Virginia Woolf was a self-styled restless searcher for what she called "a
tolerable shape" for her fiction. Although she said that a masterly
writer should break his molds callously, all her variations in fictional
design were made with an unvarying aim: she worked to create an
ordered aesthetic form that, for all its symmetry, would nevertheless
accommodate disorder, a contemporary account of the mind's irregular
action, "the rapidity of life, the perpetual waste and repair; all so
casual, all so haphazard."[1] She sought form that would create meaning
and value in the profusion of experience that was for her, although
zestful and beautiful—shifting, undependable, and sometimes cruelly
mysterious.

The search was of peculiar urgency. "It is this writing that gives me
my proportions," she wrote in her diary. "Odd how the creative power
at once brings the whole universe to order."[2] The rationale for this

quest, personal and artistic, was formed in her young womanhood. Her earliest intense experiences of psychic instability enforced her belief that the life of the mind, "the sense of the human being, his depth and the variety of his perceptions, his complexity, his confusion, his self, in short," which she later described as the very stuff of modern fiction, had not been fully realized by even such a brilliant psychologist as Sterne.[3] And youthful Bloomsbury's lively and analytical interest in visual art developed her awareness of the heuristic and emotional power of design; balanced composition could control chaotic material. She was to sophisticate but never to revoke this conception of her proper subject matter and her formal goals.

Her theory of the "new novel" is familiar to all students of her work, yet it is still of interest to see it prefigured clearly in her first reviews, written years before the appearance of her first book. Like Proust whom she admired, and Joyce whom she praised, attacked, and envied, she saw very early in her own development that the quick of the mind offered the novelist a rich new world to realize. In 1917, she wrote: "There are an astonishing number of things that never get into novels at all and yet are the salt of life."[4] And in 1927, in a more well-known piece, she was still recommending that the modern novelist should

> dramatize some of the influences which play so large a part in life, yet have so far escaped the novelist—the power of music, the stimulus of sight, the effect on us of the shape of trees or the play of colour, the emotions bred in us by crowds and the hatreds which come so irrationally in certain places or from certain people, the delight of movement and the intoxication of wine.[5]

Given this change of material, she argued, other changes must follow; fictional form must alter. Excited by the seeming inconclusiveness of Russian fiction, she pondered the question, theorizing that the new outline of form must come from an accent and emphasis on points of interest hitherto ignored.

"Modern Fiction" appeared in 1919, after her own major mutation from conventional narrative technique had been achieved in the associational sketches of *Monday or Tuesday,* but the principles of its method had been set forth in her private letters and her public reviews for over fifteen years. As early as 1904 in her first published book review, eleven years before the appearance of her first novel, *The Voyage Out,* she began with this definition of the work of William Dean Howells: "Mr. Howells is the exponent of the novel of thought as distinct from the novel of action. Men interest him primarily as thinking, not as doing, animals." And she closed the review, after slighting the plot, by adding this praise: "However, the mere plot is not essential to a book which treats with such fineness of subtler things."[6] In 1905, she wrote patronizingly of "the type of writer . . . who can dispose of the difficulties that are necessary to make a plot."[7] Here and elsewhere she defined the term inadequately and narrowly in context as a well-made action, dependent for its crises on conventional social values, often a story "which does not harrow our feelings unduly because we know it will all be solved happily on the final page" when "the sound of wedding bells is the signal for a general handshaking, and we feel that we can all depart in a state of mild felicity."[8] In the fall of 1908, she wrote airily to Lytton Strachey: "Plots don't matter."[9]

Two years later she asserted in print that what was wanted by the contemporary reader was not the elaborate circumstantial account of the Victorian novel, but a selective rendering of the brain and the view of life. Believing this, she argued as early as 1916 for the historical necessity of formal experiment in poetry and in prose. In fact, she suggested a wedding of the genres. She denied that such exploration stemmed from either a shallow impatience with tradition or a failure of artistic power, explaining that "it springs rather from the belief that there is a form to be found in literature for the life of the present day—for a life lived in little houses separated only by a foot or two of brick wall; for the complicated, intense and petty emotions of the drawing room; for the acts and sights of the street; for the whole pageant of life without the concealment of its ugly surface."[10]

As "Modern Fiction" prophesied, the shift of stress from the outer to the inner life required bold technical trial and error, not only in order to discover new methods of imitating the complexities, oscillations, and confusions of the sensibility moving in and out of the present moment, but in order to develop new methods of creating the sympathy, expectation, and emotional climax that form the counterbalancing fictional design. Again like Joyce and Proust, she worked to build a structure that would give meaningful shape to this mental experience without belying its intrinsic timeless shapelessness.

Although writing at a time when fiction was becoming, in her critical view, chaotic and formless, she insisted that the novelist must bring to bear on life's "tumultuous and contradictory emotions the generalizing and simplifying power of a strict and logical imagination. Tumult is vile; confusion is hateful; everything in a work of art should be mastered and ordered."[11]

It is established literary history that her chief quarrel was with fictional techniques based on material values. The novels of Bennett, Galsworthy, and Wells seemed to her outworn, dead, and merely conventional in an age that defined the dynamic mystery of the mind as the most persuasive reality. But if she attacked these contemporaries for destroying the sense of life by the weight of their static physical descriptions of milieu and by neatly reconciled actions, she also scolded her fellow antimaterialists, Dorothy Richardson and James Joyce, for tipping the balance too far on the side of the confusion of the inner life. She judged that Richardson and Joyce had abandoned form, weakened emotion, and obscured meaning by failing to order and control "the damned egotistical self." She insisted that "writing must be formal. The art must be respected. ... if one lets the mind run loose it becomes egotistic; personal, which I detest. At the same time, the irregular fire must be there; and perhaps to loose it one must begin by being chaotic, but not appear in public like that."[12] Although she praised Dorothy Richardson for rendering states of being rather than conventional states of doing, she complained that she had not achieved the shapeliness of the old accepted forms.

Her criticism of Joyce is significant; it is the strategic, defensive *critique de combat,* cast quite characteristically in terms of balance. She praised his exciting virtuosity, his imitation of the inner life, but thought his work cold and difficult, formless and solipsistic. She did not at once see the structure of *Ulysses,* and even after a close second look, aided by other critics, she judged it swamped by detail. It was, she wrote in her diary in 1918, "an attempt to push the bounds of expression further on, but still in the same direction"—in the direction of life. She thought it had "a brilliance snatched from life but not transmuted into literature."[13]

There is no question that she was jealously stimulated and perhaps pushed more rapidly along her own road of exploration by her reactions to *Ulysses,* but its abundance of detail ordered by ingenious, erudite allusiveness was a structural method uncongenial to her. The complexity of her work comes from its economy, from the elegant selectivity of its incrementally repeated and interrelated details. It demands a high degree of awareness, intelligence, and memory from the reader, but she claimed for herself perfect simplicity. Although she and Leonard Woolf published much avant-garde literature at their Hogarth Press, she defensively made arch fun of its mysteries. Subtly asking for praise, she wrote her friend Violet Dickinson (who had ordered Hogarth first editions of T. S. Eliot's *Poems,* John Middleton Murry's *Critic in Judgment,* and Virginia Woolf's *Kew Gardens*):

> It is very good of you to throw a pound into our jaws, when you know nothing of what you may get out of them. Mr. Eliot is an American of the highest culture, so that his writing is almost unintelligible; Middleton Murry edits the Athenaeum and is also very obscure. I mean you'll have to shut your door and give yourself a quiet few days—not for Kew Gardens, though, that's as simple as can be.[14]

Joyce, although not of the highest culture by her definition, was to her often unintelligible, and his use of erudition she thought mannered and obscure. Admittedly jealous of him, admittedly offended by what she called the reeling indecency of *Ulysses,* she made stern efforts to be just. But over and above what seemed to her the narrowness of the writer's mind, she noted another flaw which to her was a matter of psychological and technical equilibrium. For all her conviction that the psychological novelist should not limit himself to the psychology of personal intercourse, she also believed that to imitate the mind almost solely in radical, self-preoccupied retreat was to lose the great opportunities of fiction. Of this matter she wrote in 1919: "The balance between the inner and outer is, after all, a terribly precarious business. They depend on each other with the utmost closeness. If dreams become too widely divorced from truth they develop into an insanity which in literature is generally an evasion on the part of the artist."[15]

Her negative judgments of *Ulysses* are of greater value in defining her own concepts of fictional balance than in fixing the nature of Joyce's achievement. The sense of narrowness in his novel is in part the result of deliberate characterization: Stephen is confined by his cold and bitter pride and Molly is bounded by her childish egocentricity. Moreover, most readers find magnanimity in Bloom's large humility and joviality in Joyce's delight in language—both qualities that for Virginia Woolf were totally lacking in the novel.

Yet what is important in understanding her condemnation of *Ulysses* is her belief that the strong emotional effects of traditional form were not achieved by Joyce. She believed that they were to be realized by the twentieth-century writer just as they had been realized by the masters of the past: by the creation of a fictional microcosm so perfectly proportioned and composed by its underlying convictions that it gratifies the reader's desire to believe in something that is fictitious, and trains his eye from the first page "upon a point which becomes more and more perceptible as the book proceeds and the writer brings his conception out of darkness."[16] The great novelist, she says, "ropes" his novel's world into harmony by its perspective, persuasively, vividly, and consistently realized, and gives the confusion of life into the reader's keeping, whole and comprehended. "We feel that we are being compelled to accept an order and to arrange the elements of the novel—man, nature, God—in certain relationships at the novelist's bidding."[17]

In these descriptions of technique and effect, we see her principle of balance as one of composition and emphasis, and we see that logical arrangement of value makes possible a climactic pattern of experience, created by human relationships, an action built up and outlined by emotional effects that lead to an ultimate release of feeling and understanding. Defining this form and its effects, Virginia Woolf wrote: "When we speak of form we mean that certain emotions have been placed in the right relations to each other; then that the novelist is able to dispose these emotions and make them tell by methods which he inherits, bends to his purpose, models anew, or even invents for himself. Further, that the reader can detect these devices, and by so doing will deepen his understanding of the book."[18] No break with the past seems recommended by this theory.

As a modernist, however, she argued that no longer could the emotions and relationships that create climactic moments be determined by old definitions of personalities or the old stabilities and values of the social and moral order. She insisted on the necessity for seeing and creating character in new ways: "nobody can deny that our lives are largely at the mercy of dreams and visions which we cannot account for logically."[19] Not only the concept of human will but that of social morality had shifted; "I will tell you," she wrote to Vita Sackville-West "about *Anna Karenina* and the predominance of sexual love in 19th century fiction and its growing unreality to us who have no real condemnation in our hearts of adultery as such. But Tolstoy poises all his book on that support."[20]

In 1918 she wrote with patience and a long view of the pressure of the times on literary form:

> It is not that life is more complex or difficult now than at any other period, but that for each generation the point of interest shifts, the old form puts the interest in the wrong places, and in searching out the severed and submerged part of what to us constitutes form we seem to be throwing fragments together at random and disdaining the very thing that we are trying our best to rescue from chaos.[21]

As the century wore on, and as she matured, she recanted the main clause, and like her friend, T. S. Eliot, described the modern sensibility as a new psychic phenomenon, subtle, self-conscious, and acutely perceptive. Repeatedly she labeled her own time as one of discord, incongruity, contrast, curiosity, sneer, and disbelief. She saw this gray climate of doubt as blighting to the novelist's power to create response. "One advantage of having a settled code of morals is that you know exactly what to laugh at," she wrote, envying Goldsmith's assurance.[22] Without either a common ground of faith or the novelist's own confidence in the truth of his personal vision, he cannot establish the crises that create fictional form.

Although she sometimes seems to forget that for the sensitive and the intelligent the times are always tumultuous and transitional, she did not entirely succumb to the self-pitying fallacy that this age was preternaturally uncongenial for the writer. In writing to John Lehmann in "A Letter to a Young Poet," she counsels: "Never think yourself singular, never think your own case much harder than other people's." And though she adds, "I admit that the age we live in makes this difficult," she offers him the consolation of a place in the long line of poets who wrote in fragmented times.[23]

What she saw as fundamental to a successful novel was a principle of belief that governs, balances, and unifies its selection and arrangement of details. Cruelly honest with herself, she found this hard to come by. The persistent doubt generated by her extreme temperamental ambivalence made many devices inappropriate: an authoritative authorial tone or point of view, fixed characterization by which to build sympathy and provide motivation, conventional chronology, confidence in permanent revelation through human relationships, climaxes depending on clear-cut moral conflicts, or, most importantly, any stable resolution of initial instability that could make classic tragic or comic forms available to her. She made use of some of these techniques in her early work, but she persistently strove to create a form that would hold in temporary and revealing relationship ideas and feelings that were logically inconsistent but true to her own perceptions and emotions.

She resisted system; she was enraged by dogma. The social implications of this passion in her work are increasingly recognized. Her opposition to coercive authority, domestic or societal, and her concern for the quality of the individual life and for the disinterestedness of the artist's search for truth were, as we know, developed through an eclectic private education. It began in childhood through hungry, curious reading under the irregular tutelage of her mother, of a few special instructors, and of her famous father, Leslie Stephen. A quick-minded critic, always easily bored, he was often tranced in his own busy, inner life. Father and daughter were much alike, intellectually and emotionally, an affinity she early knew and recognized. Their temperamental likeness unfitted him to teach her, although his encouragement of her intellectual freedom was a boon. Her studies were interrupted by periods of illness or instability and included no clear, connected pursuit of any discipline, no chronological structure within which to order the miscellaneous information about the past that she eagerly gathered. Her hyperbolic imaginative habit of expression, however, was constantly disciplined by one form of system—the rigor of skeptical, logical challenge by her father and later by her brother Thoby. In protest she claimed privately that inaccuracy is often a superior kind of truth. She wrote in a letter to Violet Dickinson that Thoby, home from Cambridge, "examines everyone as though they were in the witness box and he a judge in ermine. He is always telling me to explain myself clearly and to say what I mean—the which is always beyond me, but I have a singular genius in saying all sorts of things I don't mean."[24]

Her nature craved order, yet the intellectual skepticism of the household taught her to suspect any facile or sentimental construction of it. Dislike of intellectual bullying encouraged her characteristic overreaction to order imposed from without. In any case, she saw no place for systematized "truths" of any kind in the novel; the *idée fixe* in fiction was abhorrent to her. In reading D. H. Lawrence's *Letters,* she wrote: "And the repetition of one idea. I don't want that either. I don't want 'a philosophy' in the least: I don't believe in other people's reading of riddles."[25] Indeed, although she was a champion of the intellect, she opposed any use of it so rigorous and ruthless that it threatened humanity and creativity. Describing an old friend, long-schooled in Cambridge positivism but sunk in depression in middle age, she wrote her sister: "I can't help thinking that this is a judgment upon Cambridge generally; it's what happens if you go on telling the truth. You lose all generosity and all power of imagination. Moreover, you inevitably become a complete egoist."[26]

As a young woman she was exposed to her father's rational agnosticism and to the constant metaphysical debates of her brother's friends, the young positivist disciples of G. E. Moore. She read Moore's *Principia Ethica,* modestly deprecating her own capacity to grasp it, but she did not engage in abstract metaphysical analysis, even though she understood its fundamental concerns. There is indeed an implied ontology and a clearly realized theory of epistemology in her mature fiction; she wrote novels of metaphysical search.[27] But her statements of belief and unbelief are always made in the most palpable terms; she transforms theory into the very stuff of life. "She would not generalize; she would always particularize," writes David Garnett. "Her imagination ranged in a world where everything was alive."[28]

She held that a novelist's beliefs should infuse and govern his creative imagination, that he should focus his attention on aesthetic questions of relationship that grew out of the relationship of those ideas. To understand the complexity of her own perspective, it is necessary to consider the divided and changing views she held on what she had named as the elements of the novel—God, nature, and man.

Her letters, her diary, and the sympathetic characters in the novels manifest an emotional longing for a deity, but an intellectual rejection of orthodox Christianity. In 1903, during her father's last long illness, she wrote to Violet Dickinson: "Please ask Hester L. to supply me with a god quick—not the Christian god."[29] The first person speaker in "An Unwritten Novel," the soliloquy of a writer, describes the Christian God as an old gentleman in a black frock coat, "his hand trailing in the clouds," holding a rod, "black, thorned, a truncheon, is it? —a brutal old bully."[30] The four deaths in her immediate family before she was twenty-five, three of which were sudden blows, confirmed this vision.

An unpublished letter, written when she was twenty-one, contains her most positive affirmation that a power of some limited goodwill might exist, but she puts her faith in the renewing force of what she often spoke of as "life itself": "the only reason I have to believe in a God is that some life grows in one and outgrows most things. But otherwise—it seems to me he has a heavy hand."[31] Again and again across the natural beauty of her vivid fictional world falls the shadow of a power that is indifferent, unknowable, irrational, and inexorable, permitting by its lack of attention sudden death and all manner of tyranny.

A 1929 diary entry makes a touching reference to her childhood search for God in the period after her mother's death, but its tone is matter-of-fact: "I was 15 or 16 ... I was then writing a long picturesque essay upon the Christian religion, I think; called Religio Laici, I believe, proving that man has need of a God, but the God was described in process of change."[32] The matriarchal figures in her early novels play roles of power and magic; there is a need for them to complement the possible tyranny of the patriarch. The women to whom she was deeply attached, Violet Dickinson, her sister Vanessa, and Vita Sackville-West, stood always in the role of protector or cherisher. In a letter to Violet Dickinson from Paris, she describes the Venus de Milo as a goddess of maternal rather than romantic love. Likening the statue to three mother figures in her own life and referring to herself by the Greek word for "sparrow," she writes: "That divine Venus who is Katie and you and Nessa and all good and beautiful women—whom I adore. I weep tears of tenderness to think of that great heart of pity for *Sparroy* locked up in stone—never to throw her arms round me—as she would if only she could—I know it and feel it."[33]

That same Violet, with whom Virginia Stephen enjoyed until her marriage what Quentin Bell calls "an affair of the heart," had both the masculine strength and the uncritical affection for which Virginia yearned. The photograph of the two together in Volume 1 of the biography shows Virginia literally sheltering herself in her six-foot friend's shadow. In her young womanhood Virginia called her "a mother wallaby" and in moments of grief longed to crawl into her pouch, a patent image that requires no comment.

Violet Dickinson lacked the keen intellect that Virginia admired, but, as Quentin Bell writes, "she had a breezy masculine assurance, a cheerful imperturbable balance, she was a lofty and reassuring tower of strength. But she must have had something more than strength, a certain real greatness of mind and character. She could take mockery, give sympathy, understanding, and love with immense generosity."[34] Here was a quite human prototype of a life-giving divinity more human and more accessible than the Jehovah she abhorred. In a fairy story Virginia Stephen dedicated to Violet appeared a giant goddess to whom young maidens brought offerings all day long.

In any case, although practiced in witty irreverence, schooled in rational doubt, Virginia Woolf was instinctively a worshipper; her lyricism sprang from her spirit of adoration, directed toward the ephemeral beauty of the physical world. Yet her attitude toward nature was a divided one. E. M. Forster called matter the enemy and the friend of her mind.[35] Nature, the phenomenal world, sometimes offered her sensory and emotional pleasure that implied a mysterious unity promising release of self. Sometimes it was such a terrifying chaos that the power of art had to be called upon to hold it at bay. For she saw man at the mercy of unseen powers with death ever hurrying near, confirming his existence through his cognition and re-creation of a beautiful and decaying world: "everybody believes that the present is something, seeks out the different elements in this situation in order to compose the truth of it, the whole of it."[36]

But man's chance of knowing himself or another seems frail. Katherine Hilberry, the heroine of *Night and Day,* walks beside her husband-to-be and thinks bleakly: "She might speak to him, but with that strange tremor in his voice, those eyes blindly adoring, whom did he answer? What woman did he see?"[37]

Such skepticism of romantic love, at least of its centrality in human happiness, was in part a doubt of the possibility of full human communion, but it was also deeply complicated by Virginia Woolf's response to sexual love. Her last memoir said she felt fear and shame of her own body as a small child; she admitted she distrusted and was aesthetically offended by what she called "the profound instincts" that draw men and women together. She was always to be, as she herself said in correspondence, susceptible to female charms. Though honoring what she called the dignity and safety that men brought to the life of civilization, she found them in private company more likely than women to be complacent, pretentious, and domineering, behavior that offended her. Early distasteful experiences of forced physical attentions from her half-brother confirmed her revulsion toward coercion or capture. In early correspondence Vita Sackville-West complained of Virginia Woolf's coldness and inviolability, further evidence of her insistence on privacy. The letters that passed between Virginia Stephen and Leonard Woolf during their engagement show Leonard as a passionate man, smitten, overwhelmed, and nearly immobilized by his sense of her beauty, her genius, and her enormous power to charm. Her replies move by degrees from the stern honesty that would not permit her to inflate her far lesser response to a tender receptivity. There is no joyous sexual fleshliness in her work, although the world of the senses is keenly alive. The richest responses might be described as climaxes of visual experience and perceptive insight, shot through with erotic excitement. What is more important than this aspect of her physical nature is her wise objections to sexual domination and to the fixing and polarization of sexual roles—the failure of full selfhood and the abuses of power that are the inevitable result of such temperamental and social specialization. Like her "changed God," the ideal human and the great artist for Virginia Woolf would always partake in their natures of the best of both sexes.[38]

Her attitude toward death is as dual and complex as that toward sexual identity. She often described longingly the pull toward the still point of release from striving, that drift toward death which Lawrence scorns as the self-destructive longing for mystic unity. Of this preoccupation Leonard Woolf writes in the last volume of his autobiography: "Death, I think, was always very near the surface of Virginia's mind, the contemplation of death. It was part of the deep imbalance of her mind. She was 'half in love with easeful death.' "[39] Yet she resisted this passive surrender by recommending a vigorous struggle for perfection. In reviewing *The Inward Light,* a novel designed to set forth the Burmese faith that fractions of infinity must be joined to make the One, in a bland existence almost indistinguishable from death, she protested:

Indeed, the impression which the book leaves, in part perhaps unconsciously, is one of singular peace, but also of singular monotony. The continued metaphors in which their philosophy is expressed, taken from the wind and light, waters, chains of bubbles, and other sustained forces, solve all personal energy, all irregularity into one suave stream. It is wise and harmonious, beautifully simple and innocent, but, if religion is, as Mr. Hall defines it, "a way of looking at the world," is this the richest way? Does it require any faith so high as that which believes that it is right to develop your powers to the utmost? [40]

Written in 1908, this seems an echo of the earnest Victorian call to duty, but it is also Virginia Woolf's personal homage to the intellectual vitality that battles the pull of that suave stream. Of her own way of looking at the world E. M. Forster said: "She respected knowledge, she believed in wisdom. Though she could not be called an optimist, she had, very profoundly, the conviction that mind is in action against matter, and is winning new footholds in the void."[41] The action against matter that she most respected was artistic creation, a way of denying her own comment that we are only spectators at a pageant who must accept and watch.

Her deterministic pessimism did not preclude an intense *joie de vivre,* an engagement with her times, and a lively and intelligent search for what shards of truth and beauty there might be. Full publication of the letters and diaries, often sparkling, courageous, and wonderfully funny, will at last balance the lugubrious, shadowed portrait of *A Writer's Diary.*

Virginia Woolf did have a positive faith, shared by a tightly knit group of friends, who, though vociferously at odds on many matters of opinion, held in common an antiauthoritarian spirit and the belief that the tough-minded yet sensitive search for truth, aesthetic emotions, and personal relationships was a reliable joy. Her humor, her wit, her zest, her irreverence, her curiosity, her malice, and her powers of fantasy and satire infuse her work, have often been remarked and praised by her friends, and complement her fundamental tendency toward melancholy. Both her novels as well as her diaries show amusement as well as her compassion toward man among his peers as a creature of vanity— self-doubting, competitive, touchy, jealous, boastful, and self-deceiving by turns.

To bring the refining activity of art to bear on the unrefined activity of this perceiving and self-analyzing psyche was her goal as a novelist. She wished to imitate the constant fluctuations of the minor emotions, the insatiable hungers of the ego, the flickerings of sensation, the rhythms of aggression and withdrawal, the movement of thought between past and present, and above all, the divided mind's constant gathering and evaluation of the contradictory evidence of experience and revelation. The action that she believed most characteristic of human life was sensitive inquiry, not passionate instinctual behavior. She saw the most significant moral and social questions, not in the crises brought on by conventional sexual dramas, but in threats against the freedom of the individual search for meaning.

To cast this search into a fictional pattern she sought to combine the apparent formlessness of the stories of Chekhov, who "ceaselessly investigates the turbulent underworld of the soul," and the "form and felicity" of Pope. She searched for the answers to her own questions: how to enliven? how to compress? how to balance life and art in the world of the novel? [42]

chapter Two

The balance of art and life: definition by disagreement

In the early twenties Virginia Stephen wrote a fairy tale, never published, entitled "A Story to Make You Sleep."[1] In it the powers of life and art conquer death in a mythic, ultimately paradisal world; the two forces that she saw in conflict in the world of fiction rule there in benevolent harmony. The story is set in a mythical kingdom threatened by unnatural, capricious, death-dealing horrors—black spirits, a mountain pocked with caves of fire, and a cruel, devouring sea monster which raids the island. The inhabitants are protected by two giant goddesses, the Two Sacred Princesses. The first, maternal and life-giving, the author describes as a healer, a tamer of wild beasts, a compassionate confidante, a matchmaker, a creature of such vitality that she is "forever putting forth new shoots." The second goddess is equally magical but less approachable; her worshippers are those elect who can say "without mistakes of sound or of grammar" the moon-bright verses dinted on the tablet of ivory hung before her temple.

Although she could enchant her followers with dance and song and weave spells for them, she shot with pointed arrows those who failed her tests.

At the climax of the story the island's peace is threatened by the sea monster, but the Sacred Princesses, the goddess of life and the goddess of literature, vanquish death by bewitching him and then ride on his back, heading out to sea.

The story is a delightful translation of the friendship of Virginia Stephen and Violet Dickinson, to whom it is dedicated. But it can also be seen to foreshadow the final relationship of Mr. and Mrs. Ramsay in *To the Lighthouse* and, on an abstract level, as the allegory of a triumphant balance of power between life and art. To study Virginia Woolf's theory of fiction is to see her analytical faculties directed toward the problem that her imagination solved in "A Story to Make You Sleep."

Granted that abstract arguments about the relationship between life and art are never resolved and that the question must be answered by the artist's choices in each work he creates, yet such theorizing does have a limited usefulness. D. H. Lawrence visualized it this way: "A man has to have a gizzard like an ostrich to digest all the brass tacks and wire nails of modern art theories. Perhaps all the theories, the utterly indigestible theories, like nails in the ostrich's gizzard, do indeed make digestible all the emotional and aesthetic pablum that lies in an artist's soul." In the end he believed that the most important advice was: "Theorize all you like—but when you start to paint, shut your theoretic eyes and go for it with instinct and intuition."[2]

Virginia Woolf's working method shows her agreement with the final recommendation. Her technical discoveries were often fortuitous rather than the fruits of theory, but her critical writing implies that she believed in the image of the ostrich's gizzard, too; she was constantly describing the dialectic between art and life that exists in the writing of fiction. As early as five years before the publication of her first novel, she defined the qualities of all enduring fiction as "a sense of life" and "a sense of conclusiveness," going on to describe both elements figuratively:

You clasp a bird in your hands; it is so frightened that it lies perfectly still; yet somehow it is a living body; there is a heart in it and the breast is warm. You feel a fish on your line; the line hangs straight as before down into the sea, but there is a strain on it; it thrills and quivers. That is something like the feeling which live books give and which dead ones cannot give; they strain and quiver. But satisfactory works of art have a quality that is no less important. It is that they are complete. A good novelist, it seems, goes about the world seeing squares and circles where the ordinary person sees only storm drift. The wildest extravagance of life in the moon can be complete, or the most shattering fragment. When a book has this quality it seems unsinkable.[3]

Such subjective language, though charming, does not provide precise critical terms, but she was to consider this duality of effect with more rigor again and again. Seventeen years later, for example, at the crest of her career, she discussed the relationship in a more complex and technical fashion:

For the most characteristic qualities of the novel—that it registers the slow growth and development of feeling, that it follows many lives and traces their unions and fortunes over a long stretch of time—are the very qualities that are most incompatible with design and order. It is the gift of style, arrangement, construction, to put us at a distance from the special life and to obliterate its features; while it is the gift of the novel to bring us into close touch with life. The two powers fight if they are brought into combination. The most complete novelist must be the novelist who can balance the two powers so that the one enhances the other.[4]

To understand the principles by which she sought the enhancing balance between the two powers it is helpful to place her aesthetic theory once more in relation to Roger Fry, to review her mild life-versus-art controversy with E. M. Forster, and to examine her fickleness toward Henry James. Toward each she is contentious; she defined her own position by disagreement. On the one hand, although fascinated by Roger Fry's theories, she objected to his exclusive emphasis on design, rhythm, and texture in fiction; "he looked at the carpet from the wrong side."[5] On the other, she contested E. M. Forster's belief that fictional patterns, while beautiful in themselves, are hostile to the realization of humanity in the novel; she believed that Forster's work suffered from the overdevelopment of its richly lifelike realism in relation to its more elegant symbolic structure. One might think that the fiction of Henry James combined just that full realization of the teeming inner life and the fastidious disposal of its details that would perfectly meet her standards, but her view of his accomplishment was carefully qualified. Characteristically, her views on each man's theory are expressed through the metaphor of balance.

Every critic writing at length of the work of Virginia Woolf speaks of her important twenty-five year friendship with Roger Fry. She met him in London in 1909, the year before he arranged the widely controversial Post-Impressionist Exhibition at the Grafton Galleries. She was twenty-seven; he was forty-three. Although older than the other members of the Bloomsbury group, Fry was of the old Cambridge fellowship and perennially youthful in his open curiosity and his enthusiasm; he fell in happily with their tireless, passionate discussions of art. He was never a very successful painter, being, to borrow Lawrence's phrase for the overtheoretical artist, the creator of critical ventures in paint. Nor was he a highly original critic; much of his thought had been commonplace in French art circles the generation before. But he possessed a persuasive power to convey his visual experiences, his intellectual curiosity, and his aesthetic emotions. In the catalog of the 1966 London exhibition of Roger Fry's paintings, Quentin Bell describes Fry's chief accomplishment as that of the influential lecturer who taught his generation to look; Bell praises his contribution to the gallery-going public's understanding of design, "design in the sense of order, intelligence, measure, balance, and purpose," which Fry believed to be the primary basis of all art.[6] His education of the public taste made possible the growing acceptance of works that broke with conventional techniques of representation.

The stimulating years-long dialogue between Virginia Woolf and Roger Fry explored, as Jean Guiguet notes, with strictness and stubbornness, "the relations between art and reality, the resources of composition with all its elements; structures, balances, motifs."[7] Between them there were compatibilities of both temperament and opinion. Both artist and novelist were bored by painstaking photographic verisimilitude; both were suspicious of rigid systems and rules, yet fascinated by technical discussion and tentative theorizing. Both considered the artist's chief problem to be the attainment of balance between the order of art and the chaos of experience; both felt the common human experience of momentary harmonious and revelatory vision was one of singular value to the artist seeking the solution.

Yet it was not painting, but the uses to which a writer could put the painter's theories that interested Virginia Woolf. Quentin Bell says she sometimes mocked the limitations of the painter's silent "fish world," and although she was in sympathy with many of Fry's ideas, she was no slavish disciple, overawed by his seniority. In fact, she was capable of vigorous disagreement, writing in her 1930 diary: "Nothing shakes my opinion of a book. . . . Doesn't it somehow wound my sense of fitness to hear Roger mangling these exact values?"[8] In her biography of him, written after his death, she judged flatly: "As a critic of literature he was not what is called a safe guide."[9] His recently published letters show him, half in fun, but with real diffidence, hesitating to write to her, being overwhelmed by the virtuoso "Virginian style."

Although he greatly stimulated her visual and critical powers, there is evidence that she had early developed, for her own purposes, an artist's eye, an artist's vocabulary, and that she had even begun defining problems of fictional design in visual terms several years before they met. The diary of her fifteenth year shows her persistent interest in her sister Vanessa's daily art lessons, and an unpublished letter of 1906 describes her own characteristically competitive attempts at sketching.

> If Haldane is severe, I shall give up literature and take to art. I am already a draughtsman of great promise. I draw for two hours every evening after dinner and make copies of pictures which Nessa says show a very remarkable feeling for line. Pictures are easier to understand than the subtle literary, so I think I shall become an artist to the public and keep my writing to myself. I am probably the only living person who can understand it.[10]

Her characteristic exaggeration and defensiveness are both present in this ploy to avoid the possible negative criticism of an editor who had agreed to read her work, but the playful passage makes that same distinction between what she called "the remote and silent art" of drawing and the complexity of "the subtle literary" that was to cause the divergence of her aesthetic theory from Fry's many years later. There is much more early evidence that shows why she was particularly open to the painter's terms of Fry's lively analyses. Her three travel journals, soon to be published (Greece, 1906; Siena and Perugia, 1908; and Florence, 1909), contain many vistas composed with a Ruskinian eye to their effect as panorama, accompanied by self-conscious discussions of the relation between painting and description, and of the degree to which the writer's mood infuses his account of his visual experience. An unpublished story of 1907 has a number of passages that foreshadow her later more sophisticated techniques of rendering scene as painting. One paragraph begins: "It was a summer morning and a perfectly even sheet of air shifted up and smoothed the landscape like some subtle painter's medium. Trees and little hills and far church spires all were blunted of their sharp angles, rounded and suffused, and at the same time solid of body."[11]

Further on in the same story a lighthearted digression proves that she was quite aware of the emotional implications of fictional design years before she was exposed through Fry to Charles Mauron's theory of contrasting "psychological volumes" in narrative:

> The day after the ball is always used by sentimental novelists endowed with words for effective contrast; not only does it change the scene and relieve the strain of prolonged attention—I give away these secrets, the best in my possession—but it reveals quite naturally a different side of the hero's character.[12]

There are other similarities in thought that occur in their writings both before and after meeting. One common subject, a widely held psychological concept of the period, it is true, was the recurring solace of fleeting insights into the meaning of things. Fry wrote his mother in 1887, rejoicing that petty daily commonplaces were but shams, and that at any moment the surface might dissolve and the reality behind it appear.[13] Virginia Woolf, describing the same phenomenon of suddenly reordered experience in her essay, "The Leaning Tower," compares it to the emergence of the writer's subject while his over-mind drowses and his under-mind works at top speed. To find a self-sufficient, life-filled form for this experience of revelation was the goal of both artists, and both saw the problem in terms of the tension of opposites. For each artist the balancing of extremes afforded an image of the creative process and a technique of criticism.[14] Fry's discussion of the competition between psychological-dramatic-narrative values and plastic-spatial-formal values in pictorial art is much like Virginia Woolf's examination of the conflict between the imitation of life and the formal structure in the novel. Like her, he approached the problem inductively, discussing one by one a group of paintings; he considered the balance of each, finding unsatisfactory each picture in which either dramatic interest or design dominates the viewer's response. Closely reporting his own visual and emotional experience in "Some Questions in Aesthetics," analyzing the spatial relationships of a number of pictures, and attempting imaginatively to re-create the process of their creation, Fry made clear his grounds for finding each picture "in or out of balance" by his definition.[15]

Viewing Pieter Brueghel the Elder's *Christ Carrying the Cross,* he praised it as great psychological invention, "setting up profound vibrations of feeling within us by its poignant condensation of expression." But he judged it flawed because Brueghel had subordinated plastic to psychological values. The painting, he said, was entirely trivial and inexpressive when judged as "a plastic and spatial consideration." While finding virtues in Daumier's *Gare St. Lazare,* he complained of "a slightly sentimental attitude" toward the psychological material and of its failure to relate successfully the formal and the narrative elements. The implied story of the picture and its formal design seemed to him to compete with each other for the viewer's attention rather than to attain a congruent unity. He saw another kind of failure of balance in Poussin's *Ulysses discovering Achilles among the daughters of Lycomedon.* Fry called its psychological composition meager and unsatisfactory, since it represents a dramatic human situation with dull and conventional elegance. Although he had high praise for its design of spatial relationships constantly rewarding to the eye, he said that in this painting, art had overshadowed life so heavily that the representation of the human scene no significant impression on the viewer's sensibility.

To close his demonstration, Fry examined Rembrandt's *Christ before Pilate,* which he praised as both "a masterpiece of illustration" and "a richly varied but closely knit plastic whole." Fry speculated on the process of its creation, guessing that the tension between Rembrandt's two perfectly developed gifts of psychological and plastic vision must have offered him problems to be solved only by the sacrifice of one or the other virtuosity. Characteristically shying away from formula, he did suggest that balance or cooperation "is most possible where in both a certain freedom is left to the imagination, where we are moved rather by suggestion than by statement."

Virginia Woolf's judgment that there was a surfeit of realistic detail in the novels of James, Forster, and Joyce shows her sympathy with this recommendation of elegance. Fry's insistence on a necessary congruence between the interest of the psychological narrative and the spatial pattern recalls both her term "the single vision," and her concern for the right relationship between plot and structure. In the first phase of her work her own technique was progressively economical in the interests of achieving this fusion.

Yet such similarity did not go the whole way as a working theory for fiction; Virginia Woolf was keenly aware of the elements in the novel not present in the visual arts—time, climactic emotional pattern, and questions of human conduct. She was obliged to construct a view that went beyond this study of the problems of visual design, although Fry thought it quite sufficient for prose. To him the "idea" behind a painting was the artist's insight into the underlying form of the natural reality; but for her, many "ideas" of fiction lay outside the scope of this concept.

To compare Virginia Woolf's fully developed if deliberately unsystematic theory of fiction with the rapidly abandoned suggestions about the novel in Fry's "Some Questions in Aesthetics" is to see how far beyond his experimental musings on literature the practical problems of her own fluid subject matter forced her. Many of Fry's theories were too exclusively concerned with pattern to be of use; he defined the pure aesthetic emotion as "the effects of sensations *in their relations*" [italics added] and complained that the novel was choked with such extraneous matters as "criticisms of life, of manners or of morals," making extraordinarily difficult the aesthetic discussion of its formal relationships.[16] "How far, he would ask, could literature be considered an art? Writers lacked conscience; they lacked objectivity; they did not treat words as painters treat paint. . . . Writers were moralists; they were propagandists and 'propaganda' shuts off the contemplative penetration of life before it has found the finer shades of significance."[17] He seized with pleasure on the suggestion of Charles Mauron that the novelist, transporting the idea of volume "from the domain of space to the domain of the spirit," could then work architectonically with emotional or "psychological volumes."[18]

Practically applying a similar abstraction—that novelistic form is created by placing certain emotions in the right relationship to each other—Virginia Woolf experimented with emotional fluctuation as structure. But disagreeing with Fry as to the relevance of "meaning" in art, she believed that fundamental assumptions about life were central to the novel's form; she worked out the term "perspective" as a principle of design that infused human values into the writer's selection and composition without the direct transposition of ideas into equivalents in fictional reality. It is not the similarity of their views but her sophistication of Fry's theory of design to include meaning and flux that is of greatest interest.

She said she was not trying to tell a story; Fry, too, was frankly hostile to "the story-telling spirit in art." In discussing "pure art," Fry in his middle period jettisoned the subject matter, declaring that the aesthetic emotion was an emotion about *form*, a response unrelated to the instinctual life. He makes this point most clear in *The Artist and Psychoanalysis*, his patient but firm address to a company of psychoanalysts. His thesis is that Freud's theory of "artistic creation as wish fulfillment" is of use only in exploring the popular, commercial, and impure art that overflows from dreams of sexual and worldly triumph— the cinema, the housemaid's illustrated romance, and the penny dreadful. Similarly, the subconscious into which Bloomsbury writers "let down their buckets," a metaphor used by Forster, Strachey, and Woolf, was in their mind's eye a dark well of recall and formal synthesis, not the water of sublimation. Insisting that pure art does not offer the satisfactions of fantasy but the satisfactions of contemplating "inevitable sequences . . . logical constructions united by logical inevitability," he went on, with deliberate stubborn single-mindedness, to judge the novel's excellence solely in terms of what he saw to be design, rhythm, and texture, ignoring the ideas, the human emotions, and the movement of the life it realized.[19] In *Roger Fry,* Virginia Woolf said that his speculative genius was irresponsible when he talked of literature; though her keen awareness of structure and style, her sense of the patterns of emotion in fiction, and her consciousness of the power of design to satisfy the reader's pleasure owed much to their controversies, in the end she rejected his theory of fiction as overweighted on the side of aesthetic pattern.

Yet when E. M. Forster in *Aspects of the Novel* declared for the richness and unmanageability of life over the grand chain or the converging lines of artistic design in fiction, Virginia Woolf rounded on him with texts paraphrased from Fry. Forster's frank suspicion of perfect symmetry and his recommendation that beauty should not be aimed at in fiction although it must be achieved, roused her indignation. Forster's position seemed to confirm Fry's comment: "Comparatively few novelists have ever conceived of the novel as a perfectly organized aesthetic whole."[20] Reviewing *Aspects of the Novel,* Virginia Woolf expanded on Fry's views:

> But the assumption that fiction is more intimately and humbly attached to the service of human beings than the other arts leads to a further position which Mr. Forster's book again illustrates. It is unnecessary to dwell upon her aesthetic functions because they are so feeble that they can safely be ignored. Thus, though it is impossible to imagine a book on painting in which not a word should be said about the medium in which a painter works, a wise and brilliant book about fiction, like Mr. Forster's, can be written about fiction without saying more than a sentence or two about the medium in which a novelist works. Almost nothing is said about words. . . . So with the other aesthetic qualities. Pattern, as we have seen, is recognized, but savagely censured for her tendency to obscure the human features. . . . In England at any rate the novel is not a work of art.[21]

There is heat in this judgment. Forster is never savage; no critic is more civilized or less arbitrary. But he did write one sentence that might have aroused her overreaction: "The novelist who betrays too much interest in his own method can never be more than interesting; he has given up the creation of character and summoned us to help analyze his own mind, and a heavy drop in the emotional thermometer results."[22] His criticism of aesthetic theorizing may have seemed to her condescension even though in this passage he was referring to self-conscious authorial intervention.

On other grounds her testy tone can also be explained; her criticism of her contemporaries is often flawed by defensiveness. Virginia Woolf and Morgan Forster were friends of long standing. Indeed, letters show that he consulted her at once when he received the commission to write the lectures that became *Aspects of the Novel*. She trusted his literary judgment and valued his praise, yet because of her feminism and her touchiness, there was sometimes a strain between them.

Typically reversing herself, she later attempted to correct her reaction to *Aspects of the Novel* by proving that her irritation was aroused by his creed and not his practice. In a full-length reconsideration of his novels published a month after this attack on his theoretical anti-aestheticism, she praised his remarkable sense of design and his exquisite prose style. With admiration she detailed his other virtues as a novelist—his originality and powers of observation, his virtuosity in characterization, his gift for social comedy, his susceptibility to the facts of the historical present and his delightful power to sport with them, his honest and sympathetic mind, and his moving concern for the quality of private life.[23]

But in the end she made a damning judgment that seems to undercut all the praise; she found his work marred by his failure to hold these many gifts in a powerful unity. "We are often aware of contrary currents that run counter to each other and prevent the book from bearing down upon us and overwhelming us with the authority of a masterpiece," she wrote of his novel, *The Longest Journey*. "Yet if there is one gift more essential to a novelist than another it is the power of combination—the single vision."[24] Both her 1908 review and her 1927 critique of *A Room with a View* call it unfocused; the latter half of the book, she wrote, suffered from "some belittlement" since its symbolic statement was weakened by the increased density of the realistic narrative. Roger Fry's reaction to any picture in which the narrative detail overshadows or obscures the spatial structure is similar.

Ignoring the fact that the drama enforces economy while the novel encourages and makes use of diffuseness, Virginia Woolf offered Ibsen to Forster as a model. She saw that playwright as an artist who, with Forster's same gifts of realistic and symbolic imagination, brought the "complete reality of the suburb and the complete reality of the soul" into perfect congruence. She pointed out that such unity makes the high moment of relevation unmistakable and that it does so, not by a conjuring trick at the critical moment, but "by choosing a few facts and those of a highly relevant kind" from the start. "Thus when the moment of revelation comes we accept it implicitly. We are neither aroused nor puzzled; we do not have to ask ourselves, What does this mean? We feel simply that the thing we are looking for is lit up, and its depths revealed. It has not ceased to be itself by becoming something else."[25] In contrast, she says the reader of Forster's fiction often ask themselves at the height of the revelation, "What ought we to understand by this?" since they doubt both things, the real and the symbolical.

She suggested that the choice open to Forster was either devotion to his forte, social comedy, or a less dense account of the surface life, allowing the symbolic meaning to shine through more clearly. She judged *A Passage to India,* in which she saw the balance between reality and symbol most nearly achieved, as his most successful work: "And though it is still true that there are ambiguities in important places, moments of imperfect symbolism, a greater accumulation of facts than the imagination is able to deal with, it seems as if the double vision which troubles us in the earlier books was in process of becoming single."[26]

Troubled by the sharp tone of some passages in her reviews of his work, Virginia Woolf wrote asking Forster how the articles had affected him. He promptly replied, addressing himself first to her judgments of *Aspects of the Novel:*

> Dear Virginia:
> No, your article did not distress or hurt me at all. My reactions to it were a certain liveliness and vulgarity. When you praised (and you did so often, delightfully, persuasively) I felt "She's right, by Jove," and when you did not, I felt "She's wrong."[27]

In contrast his response to her analysis of his fiction was not a contradiction to her judgment. Although he believed his method "right," he acknowledged his gratitude for her views and voiced his private dissatisfaction with his own work:

My reactions to your article on my novels were, as you know, very different—indeed reactions isn't the word quite, for the article still seems, as it seemed, a profound analysis of the hindrances that beset me, together with much first hand help which I'm hoping to use.[28]

For reasons of his own he did not use it: Forster wrote no more novels. To work in the direction of greater coordination would have falsified his fictional worlds. The characters are often unhinged by the moment of revelation, since it simultaneously offers a confusing glimpse of life's richness and the sense of their own failure of vitality. Unable to make use of their insights, they fall back into the doubleness, chaos, and self-deception of ordinary life. Greater lucidity of vision would belie their experiences. The meaning behind Forster's momentarily lifted veil is not clouded by a surfeit of mundane detail but by Forster's insistence that there are no clear-cut answers. Virginia Woolf had a similar sense of a chaotic and indifferent reality that brooded over existence and "the moments of being" in her novels are rarely resolving experiences. She was severe on Forster here because he was dealing with technical and metaphysical questions similar to her own. The recommendation that he settle for social comedy is a little like her suggestion that T. S. Eliot, had he not been a poet, would have been a splendid bank manager.

Generously and admiringly, Forster always encouraged his friend's explorations in the interest of formal unity: "You're in a very special position, I feel; you seem to be experimenting in the direction of poetry, and might carry fiction into a region where it will glow and contract. If you accomplish this, it would really be tremendous; indeed the last three books, remembered all together, have the air of a concerted advance."[29] In the Rede Lecture, however, he asserted that the strictness of the form entailed an inevitable loss of humanity. "Holding on with one hand to poetry, she stretches and stretches to grasp things which are best gained by letting go of poetry. She was quite right to cling to her specific gift, even if this entailed sacrificing something else vital to her art."[30] In the end, the mutual criticisms of these two friends are mirror images, although Forster's is less arbitrary. Virginia Woolf found Forster's novels lacking in a sense of conclusiveness because of their expansive sense of life; he found her novels restricted in their sense of life by their poetic economy.

In preferring H. G. Wells' unflagging, disordered gusto to the measured poise of Henry James, Forster pronounced the same kind of sentence on James' work as he had passed on Virginia Woolf's: "Beauty has arrived but in too tyrannous a guise."[31] One would at once conclude, if logic were not so rarely the controlling force of such critical confrontations, that Virginia Woolf, having scolded Forster for his cavalier attitude toward beauty in the novel, would have emerged as the heaven-sent champion of Henry James. Like him she revered the sensibility that "converts the very pulses of the air into revelations"; like him she early fixed on the inner life as the ground of action for her own fiction.[32] Both novelists addressed themselves to the task of rendering with intensity what James called "felt life" and to mastering and ordering the flow of consciousness by an elegant architectural competence. One could develop a theoretical argument for their artistic compatibility, but although Virginia Woolf unfailingly acknowledged that James was "a great writer . . . a great artist," honoring him repeatedly for his "rare, high conscientiousness . . . his singular power of relating silent conflict . . . and his exquisite felicity of word and thought," she could and did follow such tributes with attack, often, ironically enough, in the same scornful phrases which were later to be directed against her own novels.[33] At twenty-three, reviewing *The Golden Bowl* with a condescension unbecoming a neophyte, she wrote:

> For all the skill and care that have been spent on them, the actors remain but so many distinguished ghosts. We have been living with thoughts and emotions, not with live people. . . . We do not count Mr. James's characters among the creatures of our brains, nor can we read his books easily and without conscious effort.[34]

She called herself "a fickle Jacobean," one of those admirers who awaken in the dead of the night to experience "an inexplicable lapse of enthusiasm . . . when from the extreme of admiration they turn to something like contempt."[35] Diary entries show her in mid-sentence shifting from awe to irritation. Praise of his intellectual vitality is cut short by laughter at his effete characters. Her feelings were always ambivalent toward both the man and his work.

The Stephen children had known James from their childhood; he was, as Leonard Woolf verifies, an intimate friend of Sir Leslie Stephen and a frequent visitor to their Hyde Park home when their mother was

alive. Consequently, "that courtly, worldly, sentimental old gentleman," as Virginia Woolf described him in 1921, was a member of the
authoritarian generation from which she and her circle were irrevocably
estranged.[36] In 1918, after visiting some old family friends, she wrote
with horror to Vanessa of their "mummified respectability":

> I saw our entire past alive and incredibly the same as ever . . . all
> dressed up so irreproachably, so nice, kind, respectable, so insuf-
> ferable—you remember the kind of politeness and little jokes and
> all the deference and opening doors for one, and looking as if the
> mention of the w.c. even would convey nothing whatever to
> them.[37]

Yet the rebellious friends of her youth had been excited by James;
his novels had been the fad of Cambridge at the turn of the century.
The Apostles, according to Leonard Woolf, played at seeing the world
as a Jamesian phantasmagoria; they took him up with delight, because
"the niceties and subtleties of his art and his psychology belonged to
the moment of revolt," but they were also aware that James was never
on their side in that revolt.[38] Virginia Woolf's curious blend of homage
and disrespect springs in part from the doubleness of the Cambridge-
Bloomsbury view of James.

James was equally distanced from the young iconoclasts; shocked by
the Stephen girls and their friends, he confided to Sydney Waterlow
that "he was uneasy in not finding in them the standard of lady-like life
and manners which belonged to Hyde Park Gate and the houses and
their inhabitants in *The Wings of the Dove* or *The Golden Bowl.*"[39]

In a letter written August 27, 1907, when both James and the
Stephen girls were summering at Rye, Virginia Stephen mingled her
mockery of James' decorum with a reluctant awe of his eminence. Her
account of the Jamesian discourse sounds like a speech by a stammering
Wilkins Micawber, but somewhat fictionalized or no, on this occasion a
new writer looks at the public figure of an old one:

> Henry James fixed me with his staring blank eye, it is like a child's
> marble, and said "My dear Virginia, they tell me, they tell me, they
> tell me, that you—as indeed being your father's daughter, nay your
> grandfather's grandchild, the descendant I may say of a century, of
> a century, of quill pen and ink, ink, inkpots, yes, yes, yes, they tell

me, a h m m m, that you, that you *write,* in short." This went on
in the public street, while we all waited, as farmers wait for the hen
to lay an egg—do they? nervous, polite, and now on this foot, now
on that. I felt like a condemned person, who sees the knife drop
and stick and drop again. Never did any woman hate "writing" as
much as I do. But when I am old and famous I shall discourse like
Henry James.[40]

Eight years later, with even greater flippancy and irreverence, she wrote
to Lytton Strachey: "Please tell me the merit you find in Henry James,
I have disabused Leonard of him; but we have his works here, and I
read and I can't find anything but faintly tinged rose water, urbane and
sleek, but vulgar and pale as E. F. Is there really any sense to it? I
admit I can't be bothered to sniff out his meaning when it's very
obscure."[41] Yet in reviews of 1917, 1919, and 1920 she showed her
unmistakable gratitude for his powers—for the majestic tide of his
prose, and for his unmatched talent for disposing details so as to reveal
the dimensions of the whole in quite the richest of lights. David Garnett
records that at one time she kept an autographed framed portrait of
James on her writing desk.

Was there indeed any center to these contradictory responses? And
what light do these discriminations and fluctuations shed on her own
theories and methods? Why did she not experience and profess a
greater sympathy for a brilliant technician, passionately devoted, like
herself, to the intensification and enlargement of life in the novel?

For all her admiration of James' finesse and dedication, Virginia
Woolf found major faults in his work: she believed his sense of the life
he was recording was imperfect; she believed his novels too rigid in
design, too oppressed by the narrator's implicit presence, too wearying
in detail; she found the emotion essential to form, according to her
theory of fiction, weakened by the reader's consciousness of the
writer's ingenuity.

Her first quarrel with James was with his use of his raw material. He
believed, as he wrote William Dean Howells, that a novelist lives "on
manners, customs, usages, habits, forms . . . all those things mannered
and established."[42] Yet Virginia Woolf thought that by failing to understand the customs of English society he had ended in "exaggerating
the English culture, the traditional English good manners, and stressing

too heavily or in the wrong places those social differences which, though the first to strike the foreigner, are by no means the most profound."[43] She granted him "an enormous, sustained, increasing and overwhelming love for life," but the rendering of that life suffered, in her eyes, from "a perpetual distortion of values, that obsession with old houses, the glamour of great names."[44] Because his values seemed warped, she found the perspective and relationships wrong, the characters anemic. To her James' characters seemed "somehow tainted with the determination not to be vulgar; they are, as exiles tend to be, slightly parasitic; they have an enormous appetite for afternoon tea; their attitude not only to furniture but to life is more that of the appreciative collector than that of the undoubting possessor."[45] This seems a clear case of a critic refusing to grant an artist his subject; it was just this faintly absurd uneasiness of cultural disorientation that James was at such pains to realize.

In this complex matter of what Virginia Woolf frankly allowed to be her distaste for James' overrefinement, she could not be perfectly just to the courtly gentleman who, as she described him, was "very highly American . . . in the determination to be highly bred, and the slight obtuseness as to what high breeding is."[46] But her judgments of the form and the style of his work and her examinations of the relationship between art and life in his novels were less tinged with disdain and more revealing of her own aesthetic principles. Reviewing Joseph Warren Beach's *The Method of Henry James* in 1918, she suggested that "the important side" of James as a writer would best be understood by reading his description of his design for *The Awkward Age*. James, drawing for the mind's eye "the neat figure of a circle consisting of a number of small rounds dispersed at equal distances about a central object," says (and Virginia Woolf quotes him in her review): "The central object was my situation, my subject in itself, to which the thing would owe its title, and the small rounds represented so many distinct lamps, as I like to call them, the function of each one of which would be to light with all due intensity one of its aspects."[47]

Four months later Virginia Woolf wrote in her essay, "Modern Fiction," the too often quoted sentence: "Life is not a series of gig-lamps symmetrically arranged."[48] It is easy to read this as a repudiation of James' "neat circle." Why the firm rejection of the concept? She had pled for symmetry in the novel; she herself used the metaphor of completing a circle when she finished a book. Moreover, she herself was to group her characters so that the lights of their minds shone upon each other. But there was a critical difference in their underlying assumptions about human relations that made the pattern and the climax of a drama of consciousness profoundly different for each writer. In a James novel the complex central situation is at last illuminated; the chief characters come to understand themselves and each other better. The progress of this gradual enlightenment is the action; the moment of understanding is the climax. There is a right action to be taken or to be rejected; the human will has some scope, however stringently restricted; there is a story, as James said, for story's sake, in the arrival at revelation. But for Virginia Woolf the human personality was not stable enough to offer or to experience ultimately dependable insight. Lily Briscoe thinks: "The great revelation had never come. The great revelation perhaps never did come. Instead there were little daily miracles, illuminations, matches struck unexpectedly in the dark."[49] When Lily's high moment of vision does arrive, it is a fleeting glimpse of the brilliance, power, and beauty of life itself, momentarily harmonized by art; it is a release of understanding, richly ambiguous, promising nothing, changing nothing. Henry James works to create a climactic rising action that, although powerfully affected by the irrational and intuitive, moves on the plane of conscious rational search. For Virginia Woolf, who sees life as a flux, "all so casual, all so haphazard," a patterned arrangement is only possible on the less stable level of experienced images, aesthetically rather than dramatically coherent.

She finds James' fictional world to be "a museum," as she wrote Roger Fry on August 29, 1921, a museum "vast and silent and infinitely orderly and profoundly gloomy" where "every knob shines."[50] Her diary entries and her reviews of James' novels, therefore, argue against his carefully contrived plots:

> Either through a feeling of timidity or prudery or through a lack of imaginative audacity, Henry James diminishes the interest and importance of his subject in order to bring about a symmetry which is dear to him. This his readers resent. We feel him there, as the suave showman, skilfully manipulating his characters; nipping, repressing; dexterously evading and ignoring, where a writer of greater

depth or natural spirits would have taken the risk which his material imposes, let his sails blow full and so, perhaps, achieved symmetry and pattern, in themselves so delightful, all the same.[51]

This advice seems remarkably like Forster's recommendations, that very counsel which she had in her review of *Aspects of the Novel* rebuked as careless. But in practice she was not inconsistent; she let the sails blow in the plot of search for meaning and tried to achieve "the delightful pattern" in the poetic structure. Like Roger Fry, she argued both for form and for the lifelike departure from form.

She admits that "the only real *scholar* in the art" beats the amateurs, but simultaneously quotes those who protest that James lost as much by his devotion to his art as he gained.[52] His virtuosity seemed to her to undercut the crises of emotion by its impressive manipulation of the characters.

She saw further imbalance. Using, even in those pre-Fry days, a figure of speech from the art of painting, she complained in her review of *The Golden Bowl* of a wearying surfeit of detail, the "overburdened style" that she thought was the enemy of the novel's formal power:

> The effect of all this marvelous accumulation of detail—all of it doubtless true, all there to see if we look close enough—obscures the main outlines. Mr. James is like an artist who, with a sure knowledge of anatomy, paints every bone and muscle in the human frame; the portrait would be greater as a work of art if he were content to say less and suggest more.[53]

James accuses himself of occasional overtreatment, but he was always engaged, he said, in "chemical reductions and condensations."[54] He had suggested with great courtesy to Wells that selection must follow saturation; Virginia Woolf believed that he had not sufficiently taken his own advice. And his composure and artistry, to which she could hardly object for their own sakes, she damned for their self-consciousness.

Almost all of her lapses into genuine contempt for James are related to his American class consciousness or to his traditionalism. The traditionalism of his values, of course, shaped what was traditional in his fictional form—chiefly the detailed materialism of his social worlds and the solid plots resolved by sacrificial acts of will. The first was unsuitable for the country of Virginia Woolf's visionary imagination; the second she described as action that demonstrates "the evils of unselfishness."[55] The refusal to immolate oneself before the Victorian altar to selfless nobility seemed to her generation the higher morality.

Yet her occasional extremes of admiration must be accounted for. She did profit from his search "to find an equivalent for the processes of the mind, to make concrete a mental state," as did many writers who also denied him.[56] Her carefully delineated dissatisfaction with the novels of James, and of Joyce as well, resulted from their closeness to her own subject matter and their distance from the values that controlled her perspective. She found James' fiction too artful in its ordering of human experience and Joyce's account too disordered in its lifelike imitation of thought's confusion. Her final judgment of both men's achievements were made by the standards of her own concept of balance.

That goal was reexamined in constant theoretical discussions with Fry and the modern painters who were her friends, although she often wondered whether "the most successful work is not done almost instinctively."[57] Her conviction grew, however, that only the practicing artist could convey the understanding of the difficult search for technique: "It seems impossible for anyone who is not dealing with the problems of art to know the nature of them; or—and this is of greater importance—to have a lively enough passion for the artist's view to be in sympathy with it."[58] Her criticism was designed to acquaint the public with the novelist's view of the novel, reliving his search to master and order his experience.

chapter Three

The artist as critic: judging the balance

Virginia Woolf thought Roger Fry an admirable critic because he could make the layman see in a painting the crucial choices of the artist; he pointed out harmonies, patterns, and happy deviations from patterns. What was most significant, he could convey to his audience a sense of the balanced relationships and the inevitable sequences of line and mass that he believed to be the prime source of aesthetic pleasure. In her Roger Fry Memorial Address she describes his lecturing method— seeing, pointing, reasoning, using his own experience as a painter to re-create the canvas in the making. She praised his sensitivity, his honesty, and his avoidance of fixed ideas.

Believing as Fry did that the understanding and enjoyment of art are among the most profound and enduring pleasures that life has to give, Virginia Woolf worked in the same way to make the common reader understand the intricate process of writing a novel. Her view was that of the practicing writer, but she assumed the role of a knowledgeable reader who did not want to fetter a fellow reader's judgment but to open his eyes and to increase his pleasure. She warned him against critical dogmatists and urged his sympathy for the novelist. Her declared passion for the artist's view was as keen as that of Henry James, and it infused her definition of modern criticism. The modern critic, she says, discards all "barren" laws of art and all "sweeping and sterile" systems in order "to enter the mind of the writer, to see the work of art itself, and to judge how far each writer had succeeded in his aim." She acknowledged that this abandonment of rule was itself a difficult rule, demanding of the critic the highest degree of imaginative flexibility, yet she insisted that he must use his freedom, because "to be free to make one's own laws, and to do it afresh for every newcomer is an essential part of any criticism worth having."[1]

The danger of this empirical individualism, she admitted, was impressionism, which in both art and criticism might meander into irrelevant, egotistical diversions. But she claimed a compensatory gain from the honest admission that the critic's voice is private and fallible, not oracular and final. She described this advantage while scolding Coventry Patmore for making Aristotle responsible for the "oddities" of his own judgment:

> In an impressionistic critic of the school which Patmore condemned you will meet precisely the same freaks of prejudice and partisanship, but with the difference that as no attempt is made to relate them to doctrine and principles, they pass for what they are, and the door being left wide open, interesting ideas may take the opportunity to enter in. But Patmore was content to state his principle and shut the door.[2]

This comment is suffused with her hostility to male figures of authority, but she did believe firmly that only with the door wide open to tentative and experimental ideas could the twentieth-century critic perform his primary duty—"keep the atmosphere in a right state for the production of works of art."[3] Having been an eyewitness to the British public in paroxysms of rage and laughter before the paintings of Gauguin, Cézanne, and Van Gogh in November 1910, she knew that formal experimentation in the arts required for its acceptance a climate of aesthetic open-mindedness.

So desirable was this state to Virginia Woolf that in her address "How Should One Read a Book?" she enlisted all those who read for the love of reading in the work of maintaining freedom for the author. Since the common reader shares with the novelist, although in a feebler form, the desire to create, she appealed to him to instruct himself by reading widely and to exert a vigorous influence on literature, a criticism by word of mouth more salutary than that of the press or of academia. Her advice to this imaginary "reader as friend to the writer" was to follow her own method as artist and critic—to yield sensitively and uncritically to the first multitudinous and confused impressions, then to order these impressions, seeing the book as a whole, and lastly, to compare and judge it.

Her essay on how to read is a description of how a critic might re-create the writer's processes in order to bring about a harmony between the insights of his empathetic understanding of the work and his severe judgment. Although she encourages the reading of biographies and memoirs, she warns the reader to ask himself how far a book is influenced by the author's life. Banishing all preconceptions, a reader must begin the work sympathetically. She advises him to be an accomplice of the writer, indeed even to try to quicken his understanding of the writer's problems of choice by writing himself. In reading the novel he must submit himself to the crescendos and diminuendos of emotion that are the form of the work. Then, when he has allowed some time for his subconscious to work upon the first fragmented impressions, he must experience the book's symmetry, judging where it has failed and where it has succeeded according to the laws of its own design. At last, he must sternly compare it with the best of its kind.

Here in this eclectic diversity of approach is historical balance—a romantic interest in the writer's personality and individual mode of expression, a classical interest in the work's self-contained form and its formative values, an aesthetic analysis of its effect and its medium, and a judicial decision as to its rank in its tradition. Yet these critical techniques are all subtly differentiated from the traditions to which they belong by her strong desire to be, like Fry, a critic of the work in the making. All questions are logically included in her fascination with the artist's search for a technique based on his unique vision—a technique that alone can provide a principle of selection and hold all details in the most powerful emotional relationship. She asks: How and how well does he strike a balance between the randomness of life and the formal principles of his art?

Virginia Woolf's first step, "To enter the mind of the writer," was taken in the spirit of Sainte-Beuve, to whom she paid tribute in an early review.[4] Though pretending, like Hippolyte Taine, to the analytical detachment of a naturalist of the mind, Sainte-Beuve was more intuitive and less rigid. He advised the critic "to listen to writers long and carefully" and to make his deductions with intellectual tact. Criticism, he said, for all its pretensions to the scientific method, would always require special gifts. He suggested that the critic try "to seize the familiar trick, the telltale smile, the indefinable wrinkle, the secret line of pain hidden in vain beneath the scanty hair."[5] With the same interest in individual character, Virginia Woolf studied the famous dead. Sometimes, in the manner of her father, Leslie Stephen, she made superficial cause-effect inferences about the relationship of the period and the work, but she habitually erected a writer's frame of reference from his writings and a mélange of miscellaneous biographical details. Like Sainte-Beuve, she was often interested in his companions, but for their own sake as personalities rather than influences.

Her interest in the author's life and in his friends was of a piece with a major theme of her fiction—the fascinating and near insoluble riddle of the human personality. Her talent for vicariousness was well-known to her coterie: she examined the lives of the famous and of the obscure with open, gossipy irreverence. Moved by the charm of idiosyncracy, she reported homely facts about the literary great, which, in their trivial eccentricity, impress upon the reader their human reality. The mundane details from the past, neither reducing nor sentimentalizing the subject's life, create in her literary essays a tone of mingled empathy and irony.

This method, so dependent on her considerable ability to identify with her subject, sometimes failed embarrassingly, resulting in such partisan and disputable assertations as: "No one has ever loved Dickens as he loves Shakespeare and Scott."[6] But the belletristic comments were marginal to her purpose. She raised a writer from the dead, not to express her affection for him or to place him in historical context or to explain his works by his days. Rather, she was interested in how his temperament and talent worked upon his experience. She wanted to enter his mind, she explained, as he was stimulated and played upon by the subject matter of his art. She presented an artist's milieu, not as a formative influence, but as a disorder of contradictory details and miscellaneous events—a preliminary view of his world as it looks to him before he arranges and disguises it for the reception of his characters. By reading George Gissing's letters, she says, we can visualize his "world of four-wheelers and slatternly land-ladies, of struggling men of letters, of gnawing domestic misery . . . in a design which we began to trace out when we read *Demos* and *New Grub Street* and *The Nether World*."[7]

Believing that the faculty employed at first reading was sensual, she was especially interested in other artists' habits of seeing and feeling and in their struggles to order their sensations into language. Hardy, she observed, knew that the rain "falls differently as it falls on roots or arable"; Dickens knew the "smell and savour of London"; De Quincey saw his surroundings with the diffused vision of "a dreaming pondering absent-mindedness," which made his imagery dreamlike and portentous.[8] Her own effort to find words for the look of things was instinctive and continuous.

Her method is always to relate the reader's experience with the work to the facts of the artist's life rather than the other way around. She presents biographical detail as neither necessary to the reader's understanding of the work nor causal to its creation—rather these details help us to enter the writer's mind and to see him as a whole. "A writer is a writer from his cradle; in his dealing with the world, in his affections, in his attitude to the thousand small things that happen between dawn and sunset, he shows the same point of view as that which he elaborates afterwards with a pen in his hand."[9] But although his dealings with the world are of interest because he is a man of original talent, she warns the critic that too much preoccupation with his life may cause him to lose his way. The creative power of the writer is often at work transforming and transcending his miseries. For all her curiosity about the artist's experience, she declares that life is not his master; she is always jealous of his independence.

Turning to the next step of seeing "the work itself," she abandons her discussion of the balance between life and art and interests herself in the balance between forms and values. Biographical controversy is extrinsic to this task.

> For the book itself remains. However we may wind and wriggle, loiter and dally in our approach to books, a lonely battle awaits us at the end. There is a piece of business to be transacted between writer and reader before any further dealings are possible, and to be reminded in the middle of this private interview that Defoe sold stockings, had brown hair, and was stood in the pillory is a distraction and a worry. Our first task, and it is often formidable enough, is to master his perspective.[10]

From the visual arts comes her key term "perspective"; like the James phrase "point of view," it is part of the painter's vocabulary and has a double meaning. It stands for what she saw as indivisible in the greatest fiction—the concept of value and the fact of technique. In novelistic criticism it meant to Virginia Woolf both the artist's vision of life in his self-contained fictional world and the principles of selection and proportion by which he created its form. Since perspective provides the rule for the harmony and balance of a classical visual composition, she logically uses visual, even linear metaphor to describe the effects of novels in which the fundamental assumptions about human experience are coherently and emotionally realized. A Peacock novel, although its author delights in distortions, is "so manageable in scale that we can take its measure."[11] Jane Austen, in relating her characters, creates between them "exact distances and accurate measurement" both literal and psychological; the reader sees Hardy's figure "against the earth, the storms, and the seasons" and "in their relations to time, death, and fate," and as a result "they take on more than mortal size."[12] In *A Passage to India,* Forster "builds his model on a larger scale" than in his English novels, including with its more extended physical scene a wider scope of experience for its characters.[13] These are impressionistic metaphors of effect; like Fry, Virginia Woolf is pointing out and bringing to the surface the elements of design and relationship by which effects are realized. She uses visual terms to emphasize that the emotional power of the whole is dependent on a coherent and balanced composition. She says, "A work of art means that one part gets strength from another part."[14]

In her critical vocabulary, "perspective" controls the fictional imitation of reality; it is not merely a thematic principle, although themes are part of its mastering unity. In her "Phases of Fiction" novelists are ranged, with appropriate distinctions, not by chronological order or by their common thematic concerns but by like technical problems that stem from similar fundamental assumptions about the life in their imaginary worlds. Proust and Dostoevsky are placed side by side because for both the inner life has a distinct and peculiar beauty; their common problem is to develop a climactic action true to the workings of this inner existence. If they can imagine a persuasive form, if they can effectively choose, order, and balance details, if they can create emotional high points true to the peculiar reality of the fictional world—in short, if they can realize their perspective—the power of their fiction will temporarily flout and destroy the reader's own sense of life, impose itself upon his imagination and possess it. She offers the masterpiece of *Robinson Crusoe* as a model; its perspective forces us to abandon our large and romantic view of life on a desert island. Defoe's belief in fact, substance, and utility governs the reader's emotion and his glad response to every invention and discovery of Crusoe. Defoe's reality masters the reader because all details relate to the fundamental principles of belief in the novel; the fictional form is in perfect harmony with the fictional values.

Any critic using the word "reality" must define it. Virginia Woolf most often uses it to stand for a mysterious entity that lies behind experience. But in considering the particular historical reality that a writer must realize, she defines it this way, skillfully avoiding abstraction:

> At the outset in reading an Elizabethan play we are overcome by the extraordinary discrepancy between the Elizabethan view of reality and our own. The reality to which we have grown accustomed is, speaking roughly, based upon the life and death of some knight called Smith, who succeeded his father in the family business of pitwood importers, timber merchants and coal exporters, was well known in political, temperance, and church circles, did much for the poor of Liverpool and died last Wednesday of pneumonia while on a visit to his son at Muswell Hill. That is the world we know. That is the reality which our poets and novelists have to expound and illuminate.[15]

She goes on to contrast the Elizabethan view of reality, which easily encompassed unicorns and ghosts, the extravagant behavior of a Belimperia, and a sense of the presence of the gods. Less vividly, her definition of the reader's reality can be paraphrased as the phenomena of his experience and imagination to which he unhesitatingly attaches meaning and the cause-effect sequences that he accepts or predicts automatically. A novel must enlarge or narrow, light up or darken this view by its own scheme of order and belief. To enjoy and to understand fully, the reader must recognize the writer's perspective rather than impose his own reality on the fiction.

This means he must recognize and temporarily accept the underlying values of the novel. If the foregoing discussion is in the language of ontology, psychology, and literary convention, it is moral as well, although Virginia Woolf sidesteps the word. Discussing the technique of *Emma* in her essay on Greek tragedy, she makes clear that if Jane Austen placed her characters in closest proximity in a world of narrow physical limits, "bound and restricted to a few definite movements," the result was to increase the emotional and ethical leverage of their every act of will.[16]

But she points out to the common reader that the consistency of a novelist's perspective cannot alone provide the power of his fiction. He must perfectly believe his own fictional view. If a writer develops a technique suited to the order of his convictions and his convictions begin to lose their validity and vitality for him, he is left, as Virginia Woolf believed Conrad was left in his final period, with "old nobilities and sonorities . . . a little wearily reiterated as if times had changed."[17] But believing in his perspective, he must labor so that it perfectly and unobtrusively controls the art of his fiction. Wherever he may be convicted of patently asserting his creed, there is grave weakness. She called Hardy the greatest tragic writer among English novelists, but thought *Jude the Obscure* a failure because it is too often argument rather than impression.

The reader who, in Virginia Woolf's opinion, can exert a valuable influence on literature is the reader who sensitively and appreciatively responds to the novel in which technique and belief are perfectly harmonious. And this reader is one who will take pleasure in the inevitable balance and unity of the form.

Virginia Woolf is not an obviously innovative critic; this is hardly avant-garde aesthetic theory, and her terminology is far from precise. Her critical emphasis on value as formative, on the intellectual and emotional power of harmonia, on the interpenetrating relationship of past and present, on the desirability of authorial effacement, and on literature as a source of wisdom and delight is so plainly from the classical tradition of criticism that it is of interest chiefly because of her fresh examples and her avoidance of such jargon as the foregoing. Her discussion of the magnitude of the action in *Jude the Obscure* might serve as a footnote to Matthew Arnold's "Preface" in his 1853 *Poems;* her observation on the action of *Ulysses*—"that there are not only other aspects of life, but more important ones into the bargain"—is as morally judgmental as Samuel Johnson; her comparison of Hemingway's characters to those of Maupassant and Chekhov, a time-tested critical method, echoes the reminders of Arnold and T. S. Eliot that dead geniuses are always our contemporaries.[18] But her lack of dogmatism, her respect for the common reader, and her brilliant use of metaphor create a tone and a method that are uniquely her own.

Although a literary essayist with classical loyalties, she was fiercely antitheoretical. Her criticism is never a reasoned, precise, systematic discussion of the problems of art. Her references to the past are in terms of the continuity of human life rather than of literary history. The key statements of her working hypothesis on the nature of balance in fiction come from a wide variety of essays and reviews. Her method was inductive and her principles, developed during the discussion of specific works, ranged in a psychological spectrum rather than in sharp categories. Her major statement of fictional theory, "Phases of Fiction," is largely description of a variety of perspectives as demonstrated by the works of major novelists whom she classifies as romantics, truth-tellers, character-mongers and comedians, psychologists, satirists and fantastics, and poets.

Because she defined "the book itself" as "not form which you can see but emotion you can feel," the descriptions move from considerations of formal problems to Pateresque aesthetic reveries. She was quite aware of the difference between the two critical methods. Quoting, with unmistakable appreciation, from the imagistic reflections of Hazlitt on a dusty folio, she adds: "Needless to say that is not criticism.

It is sitting in an armchair and gazing into the fire, and building up image after image of what one has seen in a book. It is loving and taking the liberties of a lover. It is being Hazlitt."[19] And of some of her criticism the reader must say, "It is being Virginia Woolf." In part she seems to be obeying Pater's injunction to define the special unique impression of pleasure. Yet surprisingly, her contempt for Sir Edmund Gosse's similar critical goal, which she describes as "to illumine, to make visible and desireable . . . the finished article," is only delicately veiled by her compliments to his learning and his urbanity.[20] For her the distinction was between the critic like Gosse who can appreciate the finished article and the critic like Fry who can appreciate the canvas in the making. Her intent was to trace the artist's search, to produce an analysis of the effect more tough-minded and practical, less intuitive and narcissistic than that of Pater. She was interested not only in recording the exact character of her response but in discovering how the artist evoked it. "Although to feel is of the first importance, to know *why* one feels is of great importance, too," she wrote in 1917.[21] To know why, one must examine technique, but never with the scientific analysis of academic criticism, which, as Quentin Bell notes, she distrusted altogether.

There is, however, no denying her numerous affinities with the romantic classicist Pater: the admiration of the resources of prose, the emphasis on art's fixing of the fleeting moment, the desire to merge matter and form indivisibly, and the elevation of the intense moment of vision. Even her cautious and undeveloped definition of the relation between ethics and aesthetics is reminiscent of *Marius the Epicurean:* "We cannot help thinking that of the two poems the one with a higher morality is better aesthetically than the one with a lower morality."[22] Most important perhaps is the similarity between her theory of perspective and Pater's assertion that it is not "fact" but the artist's "sense of fact" which reigns in his work.

In reprise, although her literary essays are not systematized criticism, they are part of a critical tradition. They examine the writer's experiences, define his perspective, and attempt to see how he has fused the two into a form with emotional power. They are not precise and exhaustive analyses, but they do not pretend to be. Her essays seek to create an understanding of works in the making written by writers who interest her, and as David Daiches has observed, her taste was remarkably catholic. In addition, with great intuition and sympathy, her criticism dealt with many women writers as they had never been dealt with before. Virginia Woolf's essays are the tributes of a grateful and sensitive reader who understands the intricate processes of writing; they are evocative, urbane, confident, and felicitous.

Her contemporary reviews, however, have a different tone. Their rhetorical position is no longer informed reader to reader but writer to writer. She is no longer talking about household saints but about sibling rivals. There are essential similarities, of course. She still occasionally attempts to guess the source of an author's inspiration, that moment of experience which began the process of his creation, and she is always conscious of the difficult work that follows this flash, but she is no longer greatly confident that her judgment of his work will hold up in the future.

There is no question that she took her reviewing seriously, but for all her scrupulosity she believed that any criticism of one's contemporaries is inevitably flawed by lack of distance and by professional jealousy. "No creative writer can stomach another contemporary," she wrote dogmatically.[23] Indeed, she did not always display the open-minded generosity she recommends in "How Should One Read a Book?" but she frankly delineates her biases. In 1918, after fourteen years of reviewing, she writes with characteristic duality in a *Times Literary Supplement* (hereafter *TLS*) review:

> For it is extremely difficult to take the writings of one's contemporaries seriously. The spirit in which they are read is a strange compact of indifference and curiosity. On the one hand the assumption is that they are certainly bad, and on the other the temptation assails us to find them a queer and illicit fascination. Between these two extremes we vacillate, and the attention we grant them is at once furtive and intense.[24]

Knowing the damage to a writer's morale, reputation, and purse inflicted by an unfavorable review, and knowing herself pathologically pained by hostile attacks, she recommends in a Hogarth pamphlet, *Reviewing,* that a private diagnostic interview between writer and reviewer is preferable to an abrasive public appraisal. Barring the unlikely realization of such an alternative, she advises all reviewers to adopt the policy of Harold Nicolson who says that he addresses himself to the authors of books he reviews, outlines his likes and dislikes, and trusts that the dialogue will be helpful to the reader.

She describes her own role as that of a consultant, expositor, expounder, a post-factum collaborator, sometimes even a frank competitor. "It is no business of ours to write other people's novels," she writes in a review of a Hugh Walpole volume. "We confess in this case we should like to."[25] In fact, her reviews of biographies and memoirs, a frequent assignment for her, are unabashedly miniature works of their own rather than assessments of the work at hand. "How it may be with other readers we know not, but with us the test of a good biography is that it leaves us with the impulse to write it all over again," she begins a review.[26]

Another reason for separating her contemporary reviews from her literary essays on writers of the past is the influence of the practical, commercial, and political conditions of book reviewing that sometimes affect even the most independent critic. As a young reviewer, her work was subject to cutting and to strictures against offending. She complains in a letter that her review of *The Golden Bowl,* over which she had labored five days, making twelve pages of detailed notes, had to be cut in two at the last minute. There is also evidence in her correspondence that some of her kind words were disingenuous, although her own sensitivity to criticism may have been as much of a censor as the editor. She is always free of humbug, but she sometimes gives guarded praise where she might have censured. In a letter to Violet Dickinson she complains violently of Vernon Lee's "watery mind": "I am sobbing with misery over Vernon Lee who really turns all good writing to vapour with her fluency and insipidity—the plausible woman. I put her on my black list with Mrs. Humphry Ward. But although this is as true as truth, as the sage said in the fairy tale, it can't be said in print."[27]

Her reviews were subject to some editorial pressure even after she was fully established and less fearful of giving offense. The editor of *TLS* tactfully but inflexibly insisted that she delete the word "lewd" which she had used as an epithet for Henry James in an essay on his ghost stories. Some light on this astonishing word choice comes from this passage in *Jacob's Room*, which was published the same year as the essay: "Professor Bulteel of Leeds had issued an edition of Wycherley without stating that he had left out, disemboweled, or indicated only by asterisks, several indecent words and some indecent phrases. An outrage, Jacob said; a breach of faith; sheer prudery; token of a lewd mind and a disgusting nature."[28] (If Jacob Flanders' definition of lewdness as reticence on the subject of carnality is to be accepted, the charge might even be made against the fiction of Virginia Woolf. She found Joyce's "indecency" as disgusting as James' hovering reticence.)

Perhaps her low opinion of her own reviews or of their subjects is evidenced by their omission from the *Common Readers*. Leonard Woolf included a very few in the posthumously published four-volume *Collected Essays* and acted as publisher for forty-six more edited by Jean Guiguet in 1965 *(Contemporary Writers)*, but there are still hundreds yellowing in old periodicals from *The Athenaeum* to *Vogue*, from the London *Guardian* to *The Yale Review*. For all the occasional triviality of their subjects, their frankly described prejudices, their disclaimers, and their repetitiveness, they are essentially sound and sensitive views. They show Virginia Woolf imagining the search and judging the success of writers trying to work out problems that are of interest to her.

Of particular fascination are over forty early reviews, heretofore unlisted in Woolf bibliographies, now to be read in the Monks House Papers at the University of Sussex. Most of them are reviews of memoirs and biographies in which she is often taking the editor-biographer to task, either for having been unselective or for having too stringently imposed a pattern on the "loose, drifting stuff of life." These questions were central to her own writing; even as a very young writer she was pondering them.

As an expositor and expounder she frequently analyzes in the novels of her peers two other problems of balance relevant to her own work; the reconciliation of superficial finesse with lifelike action, and the conflict between form and idea in fiction. The first antithesis is discussed most often in her reviews of writers with a practiced facility in plotting and style. She praises the formal perfection of Joseph Hergesheimer's novels, but finds his characters sometimes "chilled by the icy finger of theory"; for all the exquisite fashioning of his fiction, she

says it reminds her of "those watches that are made too elaborately to
be able to go."[29] In a similar vein she writes in her diary of the flaws of
a popular well-made novel:

> A moving, in its way, completed story. But shallow. A superficial
> book. But also a finished one. Rounded off. Only possible if you
> keep one inch below; because the people, like Sainty, have to do
> things without diving deep; and this runs in the current; which
> lends itself to completeness. That is, if a writer accepts the conven-
> tions and lets his characters be guided by them, not conflict with
> them, he can produce an effect of symmetry: very pleasant; sugges-
> tive; but only on the surface. That is, I don't care what happens:
> yet I like the design.[30]

Her compulsion to go below the surface and to produce the symmetry
and design on a deeper level than that of the conventional outer action
is implicit whenever she considers and judges popular fiction.

On the threat of didacticism to art she writes often, since popular
fiction often advances current scientific and social theory. Because of
her own ardent feminism she was particularly sensitive to unassimilated
convictions in fiction. Her moral indignation erupted in pamphleteer-
ing, but she worked to make it an implicit emotion in her novels.

Although she did not systematize, a classification of descending
order can be inferred from her reviews of fiction that is controlled by
ideas. She seems to have believed that a novelist's overriding conviction
might affect his novel in one of three ways if he did not succeed in
absorbing it into an aesthetic and emotional unity: (1) a strong, independently conceived conviction can create form by establishing points
of interest that are intellectual rather than emotional; (2) a strong,
independently conceived conviction can inspire digressions that inter-
fere with the artistic form; or (3) a secondhand, intellectually fashionable conviction can rob his work of vitality.

The late-Victorian Samuel Butler and the twentieth-century Norman
Douglas are writers whose novels she places in the first category. Douglas, she said, found in *South Wind* a form for expressing the individual
character of his mind. She charges Samuel Butler with humoring his
ideas until the story stagnates, but praises him for achieving shape by
another means than a plot of action:

At one time we think it is his humour that eludes us, that strange, unlaughing, overwhelming gift which compresses his stories at one grasp into their eternal shape; at another the peculiar accent and power of his style; but in the end we cease to dissect, and give ourselves up to delight in a structure which seems to us to be so entire and all of a piece; so typically English, we would like to think, remembering his force of character, his humanity, and his great love of beauty.[31]

Why, then, did she assign H. G. Wells to the second class, refusing him the same degree of honor as Butler, although Wells, too, had found a form to express the individual character of his mind? She accuses him of a fatal carelessness for the power of fiction, abandoning emotional force to "talk at" the reader. She calls him a creator with "large and slack and insensitive hands . . . in too great a hurry to be artful"; "he throws off the trammels of fiction as lightly as he would throw off a coat in running a race."[32] But she makes concessions for the energy and sincerity of his work and patronizingly adds that "with all its crudeness and redundancy, its vast soft billowy mass is united by a kind of coherency and has some relation to a work of art."[33]

Contrasts between her specific comments about Butler and Wells are helpful in understanding the difference between the eternal shape and the billowy mass. Butler, she says, writes fearlessly for posterity with very little regard for the contemporary reader; Wells harangues his contemporary audience. Butler's most successful characters, like Christina Pontifex, are rich and solid, while Wells' Joan and Peter are crude lumps and unmodeled masses. Wells' beliefs cause him to let fiction take care of itself; Butler creates a fictional world that is an aesthetic whole.

The third class of didactic fiction that her reviews imply fell, in her eyes, far below the level of the first two. She believed that the arid fiction of disciples, or "novels which are footnotes to science" are removed from life and removed from human emotion. Commitment to received ideas is a dangerous state for the novelist; "the danger of a cause which has great exponents lies in its power to attract recruits who are converts to other people's reforms but are not reformers themselves."[34] Reviewing Gilbert Cannan's *Mummery* in 1918, she describes the thinking of the writer who echoes secondhand ideas: "When he draws conclusions from what he has seen and becomes the intellectual satirist, he writes as if from habit, repeating what he has learned by heart from writers of what he calls 'the Sturm and Drang period.' . . . The conventions of the intellectual are as sterile as the conventions of the bourgeoisie."[3 5]

She termed Freudian fiction the by-product of intellectual fashion; she thought a complete acceptance of Freud's principles, particularly in their popularized form, a dangerous oversimplification for the novelist. In any case, although the Hogarth Press published the first English translation of Freud, she sometimes lightly mocks him. And although throughout both *Mrs. Dalloway* and *To the Lighthouse* she makes creative use of Freudian symbolism as it had been commonly interpreted, she deliberately gives objects other simultaneous, nonsexual meanings. "Nothing was simply one thing," is a principle in *To the Lighthouse*.

Reviewing unfavorably a novel that takes a Freudian view, she says that the author, J. D. Beresford, has acted the part of a stepfather to some of Freud's progeny. She judges the novel's unlifelike characters to be the inevitable result of its systematic psychological assumptions. The new insight, she comments, simplifies rather than complicates, detracts rather than enriches.[3 6]

She herself created characters that embody her values, but she constantly feared making "people into ideas," as she judged Aldous Huxley had done in *Point Counter Point,* and she considered the danger of didacticism in her own fiction with apprehension, believing that ideas hold up the creative, subconscious faculty. Although her first notes for the plan of a novel combine form, image, and idea, her next step is to put them aside and to cultivate the subconscious powers. For while she insists "The art of writing has for its backbone some fierce attachment to an idea," she also declares "Art is being rid of all preaching."[3 7]

In making these two statements she stands before us in the characteristic, persistent, untiring act of balancing oppositions that are not mutually exclusive but which place the artist in a position of high tension and critical choice. What seems at times to be her inconsistency, even her intellectual and temperamental perversity, characterizes the method appropriate to her single-minded pursuit of equilibrium. She automatically challenges the dogmatic extremes of positions she has seemed to support; she seeks principles and methods that reconcile extremes. Her working methods follow this pattern, and her novels dramatize this view of life as a search for balance.

chapter Four

The search for balance as method and form

The belief that gives Virginia Woolf's fictional worlds their vital reality is that search itself, whether in life or in art, has emotional power, meaning, and value even though it is only relatively or fleetingly successful. The heroine of *Night and Day* says: "It's life that matters, nothing but life—the process of discovering, the everlasting and perpetual process, not the discovery itself at all" (p. 135). The main characters of the novels search through experiences of psychic confusion, investigating systems of order, seeking a moment of equipoise that can bring conception out of darkness, reaching occasional climaxes of vision comparable to those of achieved artistic creation. In two novels major figures who are artists explicitly act out this drama. At all times the forces of dissolution and decay work against the vision of a balanced wholeness and create the urgency and the struggle of the search.

The reader's expectations and sympathy are roused by the anxious longing for revelation: "What does it mean? What can it all mean?" The points of interest, the moments of greatest intensity, are either experiences of chaos that frustrate insight or moments of transcendent, passionate calm. In *To the Lighthouse* Lily Briscoe knows such mystic revelation: "In the midst of chaos there was shape; this eternal passing and flowing (she looked at the clouds going and the leaves shaking) was struck into stability" (p. 240).

The pattern of quest in Virginia Woolf's fiction has been frequently noted, but the complex permutation of themes and of techniques of rendering order and disorder have never been fully worked out. Her dual view of both forces is a common one. Order, though ordinarily a force bringing about harmony, is not inevitably so. In art it may be mechanical; in life it may be tyrannous. Disorder, although commonly destructive, is not always so. In art it can offer vital force; in life it may be the creative chaos necessary to the individual. What distinguishes her reiteration of these principles is her imaginative brilliance in making them concrete, in manifesting their contradictions, and in casting them in multitudious forms. As a critic, she argues that the order provided by didacticism in a novel is destructive to its aesthetic power, but that the novelist's failure to find a "magnet" or organizing principle for the action is equally fatal. Although in *To the Lighthouse* the serenity of Mrs. Ramsay's dinner party is to be preferred to the fragmented emotions of the unhappy family breakfast ten years later, "the insane truth" of Septimus Smith in *Mrs. Dalloway* is to be preferred to Sir William Bradshaw's murderous "sense of proportion."

Patterns of seeking order are everywhere inherent in her writing; they appear repeatedly in both essays and fiction. "How Should One Read a Book?" begins by asking the reader surveying a vast array of books: "How are we to bring order into this multitudinous chaos and so get the deepest and widest pleasure in what we read?" [1] In the slight sketch "Monday or Tuesday," she imitates a mind "for ever desiring truth" amid confused impressions and emotions. A condensation of this action appears in "Gas," a short essay describing her sensations while under anesthesia in the dentist's office:

> As we plunge deeper and deeper away from shore, we seem to be drawn on in the wake of some fast flying always disappearing black object, drawn rapidly ahead of us. We become aware of something that we could never see in the other world; something that we have been sent in search of. All the old certainties become smudged and

dispersed, because in comparison with this they are unimportant, like old garments crumpled up and dropped in a heap, because one needs to be naked, for this chase, this pursuit. . . . Scudding under a low dark sky we fly on the trail of this truth by which, if we could grasp it, we should be for ever illuminated.

The account of her descent into unconsciousness closes with this parody of the aborted moment of vision:

And we rush faster and faster and the whole world becomes spiral and like wheels and circles about us, pressing closer and closer until it seems by its pressure to force us through a central hole, very narrow, through which it hurts us, squeezing us with its pressure on the head, to pass. Indeed we seem to be crushed between the upper world and the lower world and then suddenly the pressure is lessened; the whole aperture widens up; we pass through a gorge, emerge into daylight, and behold a glass dish and hear a voice saying, "Rinse the mouth. Rinse the mouth," while a trickle of warm blood runs from between the lips. So we are received back by the officials. The truth that was being drawn so fast ahead of us vanishes.[2]

The search is made by veering between extreme positions, an intellectual and emotional tracking as common in all her writing as the quest. As a critic she often makes a hyperbolic statement, checks herself, and rationally and soberly modifies it, yet she lets the original exaggeration stand, much like a piece of evidence that the judge rules to be irrelevant but which still makes its dramatic impact on the jury. She is thus able to project a double meaning while implying a final wise, balanced, and considered judgment. In reviewing a novel that she condemned as outdated because the author had, in the year 1920, "backed certain qualities which dropped out of the human race and neglected others which are still in the running," she wrote that before the war "life itself was a great deal more at the mercy of coincidence and mystery than it is now. Life, in short, was somehow different. But that is not true. Life is precisely the same."[3] By defensively withdrawing a generalization open to challenge to present an opposite view, she considers almost simultaneously two implied definitions of life—one of the experience that is tempered by the convictions of its time and one of the deep, universal current of being that resists the changes of history.

This technique of balancing views is used to question other conclusions less intellectual: "the young man in the chair is of all things in the world the most real, the most solid to us . . . the moment after we know nothing about him" (*JR* p. 72). But in matters of value it is sometimes a perverse avoidance of judgment, satirical in effect: "Whether or not she was a virgin seems a matter of no importance whatsoever. Unless, indeed, it is the only thing of any importance at all" (*JR,* p. 79).

Violent emotional reversals as well as intellectual contrasts form the pattern of search in the author's novels, criticism, and diaries as well. Fictional characters fluctuate continually in their reactions to each other, seeking to make dependable evaluations but swayed by sudden irrational changes of feeling. She praised the Russian novelists for successfully imitating such oscillations; such scenes verified her own habitual reactions. Her diary entry after Roger Fry's funeral, September 18, 1934, records her fear of death and her sense of the vainness of the perpetual fight against that vanquisher; the next paragraph describes the subsequent "exalted sense of being above time and death which comes from being again in a writing mood." Hard on the heels of despair, life and art conquer mortality. The Two Sacred Princesses ride the monster of death out to sea.

Despite the obvious similarity of these repetitive patterns of action, Virginia Woolf's notebooks imply that she was more interested in the differences between one work and another than in the fundamental likenesses. She needed, she said, to write books that relieved each other by changes in style and subject; Roger Fry spoke often about the tyranny of an established style. Nevertheless, throughout her fiction, for all its variety, the supporting skeleton of the traditional quest plot, a pursuit of truth through contrasting experiences, may be seen.

Even her method of composition was alternation, a knowing tightening and loosening of the rational analytical powers in order to hold back or release the chaotic, fruitful, subconscious powers of creation. Although the diaries, working notes, and personal letters are scarcely a complete record of her creative processes, they consistently describe three aspects of the writing of every novel after her second, *Night and Day.* Obviously, much thought precedes the first written notation; fluency and the amount of preplanning vary from work to work, but she fluctuates deliberately between using what she calls "the intellectual imagination" and "the visionary imagination." The second, which she believed produced "the supreme felicities," she described as that state "when the engine of the brain is shut off and the mind glides serene but unconscious, or more truly is exalted to a different sphere of consciousness."[4]

The three aspects of her creative processes are repeatedly described. Her first notes are structural outlines, economical plans of thematic and technical contrasts. They are often begun in the midst of writing another work. Sometimes they center about a list—symbolic images, themes, or static tableaux. Her first published diary entry about *Jacob's Room* indicates that the search for a sense of formal conclusiveness was an early stage of creation: "The theme is a blank to me; but I see immense possibilities in the form."[5] Although her metaphors for literary design are most often from the world of the painter, like Gide, T. S. Eliot, Forster, and Huxley, she sometimes uses musical terms in describing fictional structure. One diary entry notes that while listening to a Beethoven quartet she solved a problem of order in *The Waves*.

This early concern for a structural design that reinforces and intensifies the emotion of the plot implies that since the action is exploratory, tentative, and by dramatic standards lacking in tension, its points of interest must be heightened by means other than climaxes of outer experience. The structural form must parallel and support the plot pattern of ordered and disordered mental action. Early notes on *Jacob's Room* read:

> Reflections upon beginning a work of fiction to be called, perhaps
> Jacob's Room:
> Thursday, April 15, 1929.
>
> ─────────────────
>
> I think that the main point is that it should be free.
> But what about form?
> Let us suppose that the Room will hold it together.
> Intensity of life to be compared with immobility.
> Experiences
> To change style at will.[6]

Here her effort to reach a balance between freedom and pattern is obvious. The "room" is an image of the closed character of the hero's life as well as of the environment that surrounds him. The inner room is impervious to the understanding of those around him and ultimately impervious to the understanding of the narrator. But it is also a formal principle, a geometric shape for a series of experiences like separate rooms that are contrasted by their static or their kinetic representation. They are tableaux interrupted by scenes of flux, undifferentiated by any relative value in the revelation of Jacob's private self. The plot is "free" in the sense that it resists a sharp curve of rising action; the "form" is compensation for this laxness. The freedom and variety of the style are intended to work against this level episodic pattern, which offers one "room" of time after another in the nearly fruitless quest for the understanding of Jacob's life.

The working notes for *Mrs. Dalloway* and for *To the Lighthouse* are more detailed and more complex; they cover changes in conception over a long period. But both, like the notes for *Jacob's Room,* first attack structural questions, even though a plan for the human action is added or interwoven.

The long entry on the first version of *Mrs. Dalloway* begins:

Thoughts upon beginning a book to be called, perhaps At Home, or The Party.

This is to be a short book consisting of six or seven chapters, each complete separately; in them must be some sort of fusion. And all must converge upon the party at the end. My idea is to have some characters, like Mrs. Dalloway, much in relief; then to have some interludes of thought, or reflection, or moments of digression (which must be related, logically to the next), all compact, yet not jerked.[7]

This novel was to undergo considerable change and development, but the goal of "fusion" and the plan for "logical moments of digression" remained central to the structure throughout the novel's composition. Balanced contrast was always its central organizing principle.

To the Lighthouse was also first laid out in her diary in bare structural form: "Father and mother and child in the garden; the death; the sail to the Lighthouse." In the same diary entry she outlined the form in other phrases without changing its essence: "I conceive the book in 3 parts. 1. at the drawing room window; 2. seven years passed; 3. the voyage."[8]

The more elaborate notes in the holograph manuscript, made on three different occasions, begin with a list of sharply opposed symbols and themes, images and abstractions, standing, as the notes later commented, for the "opposition between the sense of life and fate." The list closes with the subject of the novel's search:

To the Lighthouse

Now the question of the ten years
The Seasons
The Skull
The gradual dissolution of everything
This is to be contrasted with the permanence of _____?
Sun, moon, stars
Hopeless gulfs of misery
Cruelty
The War
Change
Cleaning Oblivion-human vitality—Old Woman
      She hopped up, valorous, as if a principle
Human life [one word illegible] projected
We are handed on by our children
Shawls and shooting capes
The devouringness of nature
But all the time this frame, accumulates
Darkness
The welling wind and water
What then is the medium through which we regard human beings? [9]

These structural plans were, of course, not fully adhered to, but their principles shaped the form of the novel as a whole. In some cases even the length of the main sections was noted before the writing began.

But both before and after these notations there was a conscious cultivation of the subconscious. Virginia Woolf was quite alive to the necessity of suppressing her analytical powers to take full advantage of her imagination. Writing *The Years* she cautioned herself at a critical stage "to lie back and let the subconscious world become populous."[10] Her image for this process of creation when conceiving *The Waves* was that of the work growing slowly in a dark womb: "And for my next book, I am going to hold myself from writing till I have it impending in me; grown heavy in my mind like a ripe pear; pendant, gravid, asking to be cut or it will fall."[11] She would abandon conscious planning, refraining deliberately, as she said, to let the work "simmer."

When she began to write, Leonard Woolf said, "the novel became part of her and she herself was absorbed into the novel. She wrote only in the morning from 10 to 1 and usually she typed out in the afternoon what she had written by hand in the morning, but all day long, when she was walking through the London streets or the Sussex down or over the water-meadows or along the river Ouse, the book would be moving subconsciously in her mind, or she herself would be moving in a dreamlike way through the book."[12]

At this point she resisted careful patterning. Writing with ease on the first draft of *The Waves* last pages, she says: "What interests me in the last stage was the freedom and boldness with which my imagination picked up, used and tossed aside all the images, symbols which I had prepared."[13] The syntax of her first drafts is often like the Elizabethan prose that she read with such pleasure in her girlhood. The handwriting is almost illegible. Sentences are recast but not erased. John Lehmann, who as acting manager of the Hogarth Press for a time often dealt with her manuscripts, describes her handwriting's appearance—"as if a high voltage electric current had been in her fingers."[14] Painfully deciphering it, one senses the excitement that drove the pen across the page.

Sometimes the work was "extraordinarily unwilled," like the self-revealing *Orlando;* sometimes it was "refractory" like *Mrs. Dalloway* in which the subject matter warred with the original structural conception. But somewhere along the way, she reported, the original dynamic power of her visionary imagination would begin to ebb. It was sustained, however, by her sense of her original plan. "Doubts creep in," she wrote. "Then one becomes resigned. Determination not to give in, and the sense of an impending shape keep one at it more than anything."[15] Her most serious doubts at every stage of the creation were of the power of the emotion. Its weakness, by her standards, was the fatal formal flaw: "Directly the power which lives in a book sinks, the whole fabric of the book, its sentences, the length and shape of them, its inflections, its mannerisms, all that it wore proudly and naturally under the impulse of a true emotion becomes stale, forced, and unappetizing."[16]

She feared sentimentality and coldness equally. Beginning *To the Lighthouse*, she had worried: "The word 'sentimental' sticks in my gizzard. . . . But this theme may be sentimental."[17] Working on *Mrs. Dalloway*, (which she originally entitled *The Hours*), she asked herself: "Am I writing *The Hours* from deep emotion?"[18] To a friend, Charles Percy Sanger, who had written criticizing *Mrs. Dalloway*, she replied: "Indeed, the reason why I inflict these experiments upon you is that I can't lie down in peace until I have some way of liberating my sympathies instead of giving effect to my analytic brain."[19]

She made significant changes in the last stage of composition. Writing the final chapters and simultaneously realigning the whole, she consolidated and compressed, working for the economy and density and authorial restraint that would deepen emotion and meaning at the points of interest. The period was one of meticulous rewriting, "the chillest part of the whole business of writing, the most depressing—exacting."[20] What she called "architecting," a concept used by both Fry and Forster in discussing literature, demanded constant attention to the relation between part and whole, and was often begun as she wrote the last section of a novel. This stabilization involved also the difficult task of discarding digressive or irrelevant material, excellent in itself but damaging to the single vision of the climax.

The climax of *To the Lighthouse* in its final version is a triumph of balance, thematically and technically: Lily Briscoe is after many years suddenly enabled to solve the problem, to reduce chaos to order, by putting the finishing stroke on a painting. This moment is simultaneous with the reappearance of the long dead Mrs. Ramsay, to compose the elements of the scene, and by the landing of Mr. Ramsay at the long sought goal of the lighthouse. This transitory harmony of the novel's positive values, intuitive sympathy, and uncompromising reason, which in human form are not only often antithetical but marred by vanity, is fixed by Lily's objective art. She experiences her vision of order through her ability to hold both Mr. and Mrs. Ramsay in the right relationship. Like Mrs. Ramsay, the artist is able to say: "Life stand still here" (p. 240). This balanced climax was brought about by prolonged experiment. The problem of its formal design was complex, for as Quentin Bell comments, Virginia Woolf's aim in this novel was affected by Roger Fry's interest in and theorizing about Cézanne. She wanted to decentralize Mrs. Ramsay without losing her influence, that is, to reduce "the emotionally important figure to an element in composition (an element that remains, nevertheless, of high emotional force)."[21] And Lily's consciousness must absorb and penetrate the whole scene, yet must not overshadow the reconciling events.

The experimentation progressed in this way: on May 25 this diary entry appears: "I have finished sketchily, I admit—the second part of *To the Lighthouse.*"[22] In the holograph manuscript this includes portions of the final section as well. This version includes a five-hundred word indirect monologue by Lily Briscoe which expands her "terrible doctrine" that art is beyond the trivial business of "human relations" because it reaches "some more acute reality where it can rest." Lily is seen as "extended and freed" while painting. Her emotions are described hyperbolically: "she enjoyed that intensity and freedom of life which for a few seconds after the death of the body, one imagines the souls of the dead to enjoy." The narrator envisions the painter's union with his subject as an eternal marriage:

> It was attended, too, with an emotion which could be compared only with the gratification of bodily love, so unhesitatingly, without fear or reserve, at some point of culmination, when all separation is over, except that delight of separation which is that it has consciousness of mixing—the bodies unite, human love has its gratification. But that even was less complete than this, for who can deny it? Even when the arms are locked, or the sentence married in the air with complete understanding, a cloud moves across the sky and each lover knows but cannot confess his knowledge of the transience of love; the mutability of love; how tomorrow comes, how words and their kisses are only tossed together and nothing

survives. But here, since the lover was the horrible formidable enemy—their union, could it be achieved, was immortal, no Death came between them. It was an awful marriage, forever.[23]

It is a brilliant passage, and the metaphor for the artist's emotion is in perfect harmony with the character of Lily, and with the themes of alienation, mutability, and the power of art, but its emotional intensity diverts attention from the climactic events of the last moments. It is presumptuous to advance dogmatically the artist's rationale for such a significant deletion, but it is possible to analyze the effect of the omission and to speculate on the reasons for it. In its stead appears a passage that dwells chiefly on the discomfort of the "frequent and irrevocable decisions" of the artist. Lily's feelings about her own life and work do not dominate the final tableau; rather her distancing of Mrs. Ramsay and her understanding of Mr. Ramsay infuse her with the finest powers of both. She uses Mr. Ramsay's objectivity to resist Mrs. Ramsay's seductive charm and Mrs. Ramsay's sympathy to understand Mr. Ramsay. She is the channel for their virtues; she does not detract from our interest in them.

Every writer struggles in this way to harmonize the free movement of his imagination and the analytical strictures of his artistic conscience. Virginia Woolf's struggle was extraordinarily self-conscious and extraordinarily rhythmical. Obviously no scheme or analysis can give a true picture of creation's process; an artist cannot even re-create the experience honestly himself. But some study of her technical solutions of central problems are helpful.

She often began with devices of conclusiveness—the form underlying the pattern of human action. Her first plans are not telling patterns of human relationship, but the aesthetic disposition of parts to the whole.

Her free, unedited composition created a sense of life, what she called its "tumult and stir." These versions are asymmetric imitations of associative thinking, including discrete details of sensory experience and illogical emotional reversals. The principle of freedom and disorder that generates them produces a shifting point of view, a shifting use of time, and a dislocated syntax. The profusion of detail and the uncontrolled digressiveness imitates the idiosyncratic life of the mind at the expense of the desired conclusiveness.

The final versions intensify the emotional points of interests in the mind's searching by a number of devices. To balance what she called "the frigid fireworks" of the original structural design and the disordered account of mental experience, she experimented with ways to relate the consciousness of her characters to each other by "nets" of mutually experienced sensations and by patterns of imagery that epitomize their mental states. She uses methods common to lyric poetry: economy, simultaneity, connotation, ambiguity, expanding symbols, and incremental repetition. All these patterns create expectation and climax designed to enforce the emotion of the human action and to illuminate the dominating ideas of the novel.

This final "architecting" works to bring the quest plot and the structural pattern into harmony. Virginia Woolf praised Jane Austen for achieving just such a masterful fusion of plot and structure by conventional means:

> The mind has been conscious in *Pride and Prejudice* that things are said, for all their naturalness, with a purpose; one emotion has been contrasted with another; one scene has been short, the next long; so that all the time, instead of reading at random, without control, snatching at this and that, stressing one thing or another, as the mood takes us, we have been aware of check and stimulus, of spectral architecture built up behind the animation and variety of the scene. It is a quality so precise it is not to be found either in what is said or in what is done; that is, it escapes analysis. . . . That this architectural quality can be possessed by a novelist, Jane Austen proves. And she proves, too, that far from chilling the interest or withdrawing the attention from the characters, it seems on the contrary to focus it and add an extra pleasure to the book, a significance.[24]

When such balance between plot and structure is achieved, the aesthetic frisson enhances the emotion of the narrative.

Virginia Woolf's "new form for the novel" was not new, but a variation of the old form. Structural support and poetic device strengthened a plot line weakened by the impossibility of a stable resolution—the search for a fleeting revelation that was open to the psychically and physically sensitive but not to be gained by their acts of will. Her novels are not worlds in which one is led, as one is led in the worlds of Joyce, to trust in the rich, undifferentiated profusion of experience and to affirm comically all manifestations of human life. They are fearful-joyful worlds of confusing duality; in these microcosms is a constant shifting of time and of the center of judgment. Her method in the major novels reflects her belief that the confusion of life needs the selective ordering of art to release its meaning, but that in the twentieth century art cannot produce ultimate answers. The symmetry of an underlying pattern brings, for a transitory moment, the contradictory impressions into that balance which produces insight. And search for balance between life and art is the chief subject of her aesthetic speculations; she consistently pitted extremes against each other in the search for a tension that can hold both in a powerful relationship.

She sought an architectonic design that would master the profusion of experience and yet avoid the rigidity of perfect pattern; fictional form must be aesthetically conclusive yet maintain a lifelike openness. She chose the disorder of mental life over conventional materialistic narrative, but wanted to render it in "inevitable sequences" of emotion. In favor of intuition, she rejected dogma. She strove for the economy of means by which to create powerful emotion. Her goal of a balanced inner-outer point of view was meant to avoid alike the egotism of subjectivity and the dehumanization of objectivity. And she sought a balance between uncontrolled moral indignation and an aesthetic indifference to human issues by seeking to create a form that is based on belief, an aesthetic whole that depends on a harmonious view of human experience for its proportions.

To envision such a scheme, a traditional classical-romantic antithesis, is not difficult. To apply it as a critic to the work of others is more demanding. But to realize it in a novel was for Virginia Woolf grinding, halting, self-critical labor of trial and error. For all the brilliance of her imaginative genius, she cast and recast form, chose and shifted and deleted detail. She labored toward the wholeness and poise of her first successful novel, *Mrs. Dalloway,* and went on to achieve greater elegance and deeper emotion in *To the Lighthouse.* A close study of her first phase of creation shows her theory turned into technical power.

She always worked for the effects of the traditional novel—for its coherence and its emotional climax, but she deliberately chose material that was neither coherent nor climactic. She believed that her choice of the life of the mind widened her opportunities, allowing her to describe other relationships than those between lover and beloved—the relationship between man and "life itself," between man and death, between man and art, and between man and the demands, legitimate and tyrannical, of other men.

She rendered thought as both intellect and sensibility and paid them both homage. As E. M. Forster says, she was interested in how it *feels* to think.[25] She respected the ordered thoughts of her character, Professor Huxtable of Cambridge, whom she described in *Jacob's Room:* "Now as his eye goes down the print, what a procession tramps through the corridors of his brain, orderly quick-stepping, and reinforced as the march goes on, by fresh runnels, till the whole hall dome, whatever one calls it, is populous with ideas" (p. 40). And she also respects the amorphous private intuitions of the woman she describes in "The Lady in the Looking Glass:" "Her mind was like her room, in which lights advanced and retreated, came pirouetting and stepping delicately, spread their tails, pecked their way; and then her whole being was suffused, like the room again, with a cloud of some profound knowledge, some unspoken regret, and then she was full of locked drawers, stuffed with letters, like her cabinets."[26] In novel after novel she sought to find the form that fitted the imitation of the life of the mind, which satisfied her fastidious aesthetic standards, and which could arouse in the reader an irresistible response of emotion and understanding.

part Two

Toward balance

Godrevy Lighthouse, St. Ives Bay, Cornwall.

chapter Five

"A tumult...somehow controlled":
The Voyage Out

Beginning Virginia Woolf's fourth novel, Mrs. Dalloway, *the* reader finds his consciousness plunged midstream into the flow of the middle-aged heroine's decisions, plans, rational observations, sensory impressions, emotions, and memories—an imitated action that he has no difficulty experiencing vicariously as authentic mental life. After the brief contemplation of her errand of flower buying, Clarissa Dalloway's thoughts leave the present of the sunny London street and dip easily into the past, then move into the future:

> And then, thought Clarissa Dalloway, what a morning—fresh as if issued to children on the beach.
> What a lark! What a plunge! For so it had always seemed to her, when, with a little squeak of the hinges, which she could hear now, she had burst open the French windows and plunged at Bourton into the open air. How fresh, how calm, stiller than this of course, the air was in the early morning; like the flap of a wave; the kiss of

a wave; chill and sharp and yet (for a girl of eighteen as she then was) solemn, feeling as she did, standing there at the open window, that something awful was about to happen; looking at the flowers, at the trees with the smoke winding off them and the rooks rising, falling; standing and looking until Peter Walsh said, "Musing among the vegetables?" —was that it?—"I prefer men to cauliflowers"— was that it? He must have said it at breakfast one morning when she had gone out on to the terrace—Peter Walsh. He would be back from India one of these days.[1]

This mood of evocation and anticipation, slightly touched by portent, commands the reader's sympathetic attention at once; the confident virtuosity of the narrator draws him into the life of the novel, implicitly assuring him that, even though for the moment at a loss for bearings, he will be guided into full understanding.

But if the reader is to anticipate the form of *Mrs. Dalloway,* to be prepared to perceive and respond to its emotional climaxes properly, the narrator must in this first scene persuade him of more than its psychological verisimilitude. He must be made to sense almost immediately that the action of minds is the action of the novel. Virginia Woolf was aware of this as a central problem when she began the final version that had been adumbrated by a short story and a sketch. The last entry in her working notes is: "The question is whether the inside of the mind in both Mrs. D. and S. S. can be made luminous—that is to say the stuff of the book—Lights on it coming from external sources."[2] Clarissa's way of seeing London that morning, as she herself describes it— "Making it up, building it round one, tumbling it, creating it every moment afresh"—is a search for pattern and private significance which is the plot of the novel (p. 6).

To establish at once that *Mrs. Dalloway* is a novel with a plot of mental search, she dramatized consciousness, embedding the thoughts and feelings of many characters in the movement of a single subsuming mind. In addition, by patterning its seemingly miscellaneous experience, she indicated that its movement would lead to insight. The interplay between the confusion of the consciousness and the logic of the structure produced that balance toward which she had been working during the writing of three earlier novels. She herself sensed this new power when she finished *Jacob's Room.*

Although she had clearly described the principles and the effects of the technique of *Mrs. Dalloway* years before, she had not easily arrived at this compression and control. In *The Voyage Out, Night and Day*, and *Jacob's Room* she had experimented with techniques of order and disorder that she now brought successfully into relationship. On the one hand, there is freedom in the lifelike rendering of Clarissa's thought. Her mind stands in a double relation to her outer experience, being both distanced from and penetrating the visible world: "she sliced like a knife through everything; at the same time she was outside looking on" (p. 10). Her dual response to the outer world is intermingled with her memories, but, on the other hand, there is clear control of the mixed impressions. Her thought takes flight through time and space, but its discontinuity is balanced by the logic of the associational and symbolic cluster that holds together both present and past; morning—flowers—youth—freshness—children on the beach.   And wherever the complexity of her view might produce confusion, there is the tactful presence of the narrator to provide direction.

The effect is a blending of lifelike intensity and artful rhythm. The method is controlled economy—so perfect a dovetailing of inner and outer, past and present, that it becomes not balance but unity. Her taste as she wrote *Mrs. Dalloway* was for poetry: "It is poetry that I want now—long poems. . . . I want the concentration and the romance; and the words all glued together, fused, glowing; have no time to waste any more on prose."[3]

In these first pages, Virginia Woolf solved yet another problem that she had not dealt with successfully in the earlier novels—the clear establishment of suspense in both the inner and the outer action. Her notes show that she foresaw this problem in addition to that of the point of view. Although the power of the climaxes depends on the inner light released by events, their emotion is heightened by conventional early foreshadowing of significant moments. On the third page of the text Clarissa thinks: "she, too, was going that very night to kindle and illuminate; to give her party" (p. 7). And as early as page eighteen, Septimus is reported to have said: "I will kill myself; an awful thing to say." The note of doom on the opening page—"feeling as she did, standing there at the open window, that something awful was about to happen"—is the first of many links between the double plot, although

Mrs. Dalloway and Septimus Smith, alter egos, never meet.

In *Mrs. Dalloway* the successful balance between plot and structure, between idea and image, between past and present, between inner and outer experience, between dual views of order and disorder, and between double interpretations of characters is the result of both intuitive search and aesthetic theorizing. She brought together a strong plot of search and a well-developed structure of contrasting images and scenes by showing both as patterns on "the inside of the mind." The synthesizing point of view, the fluid use of time, the rigid economy and relevance of detail, a flexible syntax and conventional arousal of suspense brought all elements into a form that yet allowed the free rendering of experience. After instability, balance had been achieved, yet rhythm and movement had not been lost.

The power and maturity immediately apparent in the opening paragraphs is in contrast with the opening pages of her first novel, *The Voyage Out*. Here, too, characters are introduced to the reader as they walk down a London street. But an aphoristic, self-consciously ironic narrator acts as guide:

> As the streets that lead from the Strand to the Embankment are very narrow, it is better not to walk them arm-in-arm. If you persist, lawyer's clerks will have to make flying leaps into the mud; young lady typists will have to fidgit behind you. In the streets of London, where beauty goes unregarded, eccentricity must pay the penalty, and it is better not to be very tall, to wear a blue cloak or to beat the air with your left hand [p. 9].

This is the voice of the "author as familiar essayist" to whom the reader may look for opinion. One recalls her early enthusiasm for Meredith and her confession to Clive Bell in the early stages of the writing that she sometimes had an inkling of how the book might be written by other people and had to fight against imitation.[4]

The technical differences between *The Voyage Out* and *Mrs. Dalloway* in these first pages are worth noting, but the similarities between Virginia Woolf's first novel and her mature fiction are of equal interest. As Clive Bell wrote her after reading an early draft in 1909, she had already established her "power of lifting the veil & showing inanimate things in the mystery & beauty of their reality."[5] And in this first novel she realized both the quest plot and the strong symbolic structure that were to persist in her work.

Although the perspective of *The Voyage Out* is the most darkly and fearfully pessimistic to be found in any of her works, its underlying view of life, voiced by the narrator, is implicit in all her novels: "When one gave up seeing the beauty that clothes things, this was the skeleton beneath" (pp. 11-12). If there is any fundamental order, it seems to be the malevolent force that Rachel Vinrace describes: "It seemed to her that a moment's respite was allowed, a moment's make-believe, and then again the profound and reasonless law asserted itself, moulding them all to its liking, making and destroying" (p. 263). Helen Ambrose, the most stable character of the novel, sees "every one groping about in illusion and ignorance" (p. 221).

The action is an unsuccessful quest for the understanding of self and others and for meaning in a world that often seems meaningless. The heroine, Rachel Vinrace, a motherless young woman of the well-to-do upper class, is handicapped in her search by her position in a society that deliberately inhibits the knowledge and experience of a young woman. Although she falls in love, marriage seems a threat to selfhood. She and two young Cambridge intellectuals, Terence Hewett and St. John Hirst, each separately experience insights into ultimate values that represent the statement of opposites and the final reconciliation of them. Rachel's vision is of life's pattern:

> That was the strange thing, that one did not know where one was going, or what one wanted, and followed blindly, suffering so much in secret, always unprepared and amazed and knowing nothing; but one thing led to another and by degrees something had formed itself out of nothing, and so one reached at last this calm, this quiet, this certainty, and it was this process people called living. Perhaps, then, every one really knew as she knew now where they were going; and things formed themselves into a pattern not only for her, but for them, and in that pattern lay satisfaction and meaning [p. 314].

There is even the rather tentative suggestion that love, although not the love of man for woman, might be a binding force.

But the prophetic vision, the brief Moorelike "state of mind" in which Rachel sees a satisfactory and meaningful life ahead, is for her an illusion; she dies suddenly on the threshold of her marriage to Terence. And his vision contradicts hers as he sits beside Rachel at the moment of her death and thinks:

> So much the better—this was death. It was nothing; it was to cease to breathe. It was happiness, it was perfect happiness. They had now what they had always wanted to have, the union which had been impossible while they lived. Unconscious whether he thought the words or spoke them aloud, he said, "No two people have ever been so happy as we have been. No one has ever loved as we have loved" [p. 353].

Their polar views—of life as unifier and of death as unifier are both balanced and deflated of their exaltation by the last words of the novel, a final and less ecstatic view of lonely human experience traveling toward death that is seen by St. John Hirst as he sits half asleep in the hotel lobby: "Across his eyes passed a procession of objects, black and indistinct, the figures of people picking up their books, their cards, their balls of wool, their work baskets, and passing him one after another on their way to bed" (p. 375).

This is the plot—a wavering search for the meaning of life. It is an inner action, but it is played out on the level of trivial social exchange. With the exception of Rachel's death, the events are insignificant, and even her death is briefly reduced to an item of hotel gossip by an old woman who says: "Miss Vinrace dead? Dear me . . . . . that's very sad. But I don't at the moment remember which she was" (p. 362).

The narrative recounts a sea voyage from London to Santa Marina in South America; it is taken by Rachel, her father, her aunt and uncle, and a small group of passengers. During the course of the trip she tries to understand the lives of her fellow voyagers. She is for the first time roused to passion by a sudden kiss from a married man, Richard Dalloway. Upon her arrival in Santa Marina she spends some months in a villa with her aunt and uncle, making friends with British tourists at a nearby hotel and with them taking two trips, a picnic jaunt into the mountains and a river boat trip into the jungle. We are given much information about the guests at the inn. Rachel and Terence become engaged. Rachel's illness follows the river voyage and her fevered death ends the novel.

The symbolic structure binds the inner and outer action together; it is elaborately designed in its grand plan and in its related details to project the meaning of the apparently unimportant events in Rachel's quest. The structure divides the novel into three sections: the ocean voyage, the exploration of the hotel life, and the voyage out to love and death. On the voyage from London to Santa Marina Rachel is awakened from her private view of life that has seen truth only in the life of the sensations and emotions and in art. She is a talented musician. Of the rest of the world she thinks:

> It appeared that nobody ever said a thing they meant, or even talked of a feeling they felt, but that was what music was for. Reality dwelling in what one saw and felt, but did not talk about, one could accept a system in which things went round and round quite satisfactorily to other people, without often troubling to think about it, except as something superficially strange [p. 37].

She sets off on her pilgrimage; the ship itself is seen as her double, envisioned as an intended bride. The passengers of the ship offer her insight into the systems of order by which society forms and controls the individual: the family, marriage, religion, vocation, and the state ("an elaborate mechanism"). "Let these odd men and women," she thinks to herself, "her aunts, the Hunts, Ridley, Helen, Mr. Pepper, and the rest—be symbols—featureless but dignified, symbols of age, of youth, of motherhood, of learning, and beautiful often as people upon the stage are beautiful" (p. 37). However, except for Rachel's aunt, Helen Ambrose, a human goddess of worldly wisdom, these characters may better be described as personifications. Through their homiletic conversations, they teach the pilgrim Rachel of the values and potential tyrannies of the social world. The voyage section is a self-sufficient microcosm of experience that awakens her from her autistic life.

In the central section of the novel, Rachel's education is extended by characters who are the conditioned products of class, education, nationality, and of their sexual roles. The quest focuses on the life of the Santa Marina Hotel. The center of consciousness sometimes shifts from Rachel to Terence Hewett, but this does not constitute a fundamental change in the search. Terence, too, is a seeker, and for all his greater educational opportunities, his attitudes are much like Rachel's. She begins her study of the hotel's life at the mountain picnic that he has arranged. At its climax she sits near him watching the picnickers:

> She was lying back rather behind the others resting on one
> elbow; she might have been thinking precisely the same thoughts as
> Hewett himself. Her eyes were fixed rather sadly but not intently
> upon the row of people opposite her. Hewett crawled up to her on
> his knees, with a piece of bread in his hand.
> "What are you looking at?" he asked.
> She was a little startled, but answered directly, "Human beings"
> [p. 135].

The human beings are typed characters, from the old maid school-
teacher to the child of nature. These British tourists carry on their
parochial habits of "propriety and boredom," which seem futile, lonely, and ridiculous against the exotic setting of the jungle. Even Helen
Ambrose sits on the jungle riverbank in a camp chair and reads
memoirs. Terence and St. John Hirst, who insults Rachel by his contempt for her inexperience, discuss the travelers, their futures, and their
metaphysical anxieties in dialogues that are the action of the plot of
thought.

Rachel observes the social effects of both religion and art on this
microcosm. An Anglican church service fills her with disgust and horror; the timid worshippers strike her as hypocritical and fuzzy-minded.
In contrast, she plays the piano at a dance and brings a world of peace
and order to the guests.

In the final section of the novel, Rachel explores the order and
power of both love and death. Terence and Rachel are betrothed on the
jungle river voyage, deep in the heart of the forest. Rachel withdraws
into an isolated state of oneness with Terence: "But as the dark des-
cended, the words of the others seemed to curl up and vanish as the
ashes of burnt paper and left them sitting silent at the bottom of the
world" (p. 276).

Though both fearfully question their relationship and all human
communion, they reaffirm their love. But Rachel falls ill. In a variety of
ways her sickness and death unite all the themes of the novel and
epitomize its perspective. The attempt to heal her and the agonizing
deathwatch show the characters who surround her groping in "ignorance and illusion." At last, the "profound and reasonless law" cuts off

her life. At the same time her death seems due to the carelessness of those to whom her care is committed; the theme of society's failure to nurture her properly is reemphasized.

The three sections are all actions symbolic of Rachel's search for meaning; they are woven together by recurring images, with dual connotations, chiefly the room-window sign for alienation and the expanding symbol of drowning.

Rooms and windows repeatedly appear to show that the characters live in separate compartments, alienated from each other in their "boxlike squares." The narrator investigates the separate cabins on shipboard; Terence Hewett peers from the garden into the lighted rooms of the Ambrose villa. Rachel and Helen look simultaneously into several rooms of the hotel to "see life." The connotations are both attractive and repulsive: Rachel exults that her own room is a "fortress and sanctuary;" Terence gloomily envisions marriage as "two people walled up in a room."

Drowning is frequently, and not always unpleasantly, associated with love, and with death; Rachel is likened to Sabrina "under the glassy, cool translucent wave." Life under the sea attracts her in a moment when forms of social unity seem inhibiting: "to be flung into the sea, to be washed hither and thither, and driven about the roots of the world—the idea was incoherently delightful" (p. 298). As she dies, she believes she lies at the bottom of the sea.

The "Woolfian" qualities are clearly present: the weak quest plot for meaning, the narrative of upper middle-class British social life, the structural form of symbolic action and image. The themes of order as unity, order as despotism, disorder as individual freedom, and disorder as unbearable chaos have all been realized. The characters have entertained conflicting responses to love, life, and death in their searches. The book is artfully conceived and written to support its perspective, since the triviality and hypocrisy of social conduct make it a fitting medium for the representation of life as alienated and absurd. The impossibility of communication is dramatized by the dialogue.

Leonard Woolf writes in *Beginning Again:* "*The Voyage Out* had an extraordinarily good press; the reviewers were nearly all complimentary and she was recognized from the first as an important novelist."[6] But the first Woolf critics almost universally describe it by some variation of

Clive Bell's phrase, "a remarkable failure."[7] They most often complain
that it suffers from some kind of imbalance. David Daiches writes that
"there is a struggle between form and content."[8] Jean Guiguet says
that there is a distance between "the story" and "the novel"; A. D.
Moody passes the harsh judgment that *The Voyage Out* is "not a coherent and organic whole; indeed it seems scarcely to attempt any unified
comprehension of its experience."[9] Its lone early defender is James
Hafley who stoutly maintains: "*The Voyage Out* may be regarded as a
finished work of art, and judged as such. There seems to be no special
'struggle' between its form and its content; it accomplishes just what it
sets out to accomplish."[10]

How should it be evaluated? It is true that a confidently omniscient
narrator seems an incongruous voice in a world without clear meaning,
but the intellectual concept of the novel is unified. In fact, one's pleasure tends to increase with each rereading, an enjoyment dependent on
the novel's ingenuity. However, its life is vicarious, timorous, pathetic,
and romantically pessimistic, and it does lack one kind of harmony, a
lack for which Virginia Woolf's own fictional theory damns it. Her
conviction was that the novel that does not immediately and powerfully establish for the reader the emotional "points of interest" that
outline its "shape" is not a successfully formed work; its artfulness is
not balanced by sustained emotional vitality.

Virginia Woolf, in writing *The Voyage Out*, had not yet developed
those techniques which make clear that the action takes place on the
level of consciousness. In the early sections symbol and metaphor most
often appear as the perceptions of the narrator rather than those of
the characters and are consequently less emotionally powerful than in
the later fiction in which they are not stylistic ornament but intense
mental experience.

The final section, in which the main characters are swept helplessly
along on Rachel's voyage to death, oscillating between irrational hope
and angry despair, intermittently sunk in egocentric apathy, fore-
shadows the technique of the mature novels and shows that even at this
early stage she was capable of creating the wavering action of human
consciousness, yet the formal narrative method inhibits its power.

Another difficulty arises from the discrepancy between the expectations aroused by the social comedy and the universal implications of

the quest. No perceptive reader will fail to respond to the novel's heavy signals of double meaning in the early pages, but detailed representations of dramatic scenes along the way arouse conventional expectations. For example, Richard Dalloway, perfectly designed as a character to personify the fatuousness of power politics and of the subjugation of women by adoration, is a tutorial figure along the way of Rachel's quest, and as such he quite properly appears and disappears from the action without a trace. This disappearance is also appropriate to the perspective of life in an absurd world, yet his character is made humanly complex by the account of his childhood, a particularization that is at odds with the simplicity of a flat characterization. This specification of character and the tone of social comedy and potential romance introduced by his encounter with Rachel might lead the reader to expect his return—if this were a "well-made novel." In fact, Clive Bell, reading an early version, noted: "Surely the Dalloways must appear again."[11] Virginia Woolf's advice to Forster about the balance necessary when both realism and symbolism are used together may well be the result of her own failures to bring the two together successfully in *The Voyage Out* and *Night and Day*. Her technical solution was to be greater economy in the use of that mundane detail which is without symbolic implications.

Most important to consider, however, is the deliberate control of emotion by the narrator's ironic distancing of Rachel Vinrace, a character who bears much resemblance to herself. This distance tends to reduce sympathy for the protagonist in the early sections of the novel and to prevent the reader from identifying with her sufferings.

Study of biographical evidence, of final revisions, and of the techniques she used to avoid sentimentality in delineating Rachel shows that Virginia Woolf's strong desire to portray effective emotion struggled against her fear of displaying uncontrolled feeling. Her early correspondence with Violet Dickinson shows both the depth of her affections and the screen behind which she hid them. Writing to her friend of *The Voyage Out* in the earliest days of its long composition, she commented:

> As for the work of my imagination, I turn hot and cold over it, and my friends tell me that it is no good for me to write a novel. They

say my creatures are all cold-blooded like those [illegible] Herrings. But you don't, my Violet, do you? Ever since we two trod the groves together you have seen that my passion was for love and humanity; though it has had to kindle through green depths of water.[12]

When the book was at last set in type, she attempted suicide and suffered a mental collapse that lasted two years. Both Leonard Woolf and Quentin Bell describe its severe symptoms in detail. One factor in its onset was her fear of the public exposure of her private emotions; in fact, a letter from a family friend to Violet Dickinson, written at the time of the attempted suicide, attributes her turmoil to the imminent publication of *The Voyage Out:* "It was a huge dose of veronal she took at Brunswick Square and she was only saved by a stomach pump being used at once. It is the novel which has broken her up. She finished it and sent the proofs back for correction and suddenly went into a panic—couldn't sleep and thought everyone would jeer at her."[13] This is a layman's simplification of a complex illness, but the panic indeed due in part to her fear of negative criticism and in part to her fear of revealing inhibited emotions, as Leonard Woolf verifies. Her diary entry while rereading *The Voyage Out* several years after it was published—and it was not published until she was well again—reads: "Is the time coming when I can endure to read my own writing in print without blushing—shivering and wishing to take cover?"[14] In her essay, "The Patron and the Crocus," she appeals to the critic to lend the writer support by bracing him against sentimentality on the one hand and a craven fear of expressing his feelings on the other. "It is worse, he will say, and perhaps more common, to be afraid of feeling than to feel too much."[15] Yet she believes in the aesthetic power of restraint, advising that pathos is more moving in the midst of reserve; "the poet's sudden emotion tells the more when it is obviously not good manners to talk about oneself."[16] It was this axiom that was to govern the authorial intrusions of *Jacob's Room*.

One method of distancing the character of Rachel is the initial point of view from which she is observed; she is first seen through the eyes of her aunt, Helen Ambrose, "who looked straight and considered what she saw" (p. 14). Helen emphasized Rachel's socially conditioned naiveté, important to the feminist theme, but she also makes unsympathetic observations about her niece. She thinks with dismay of spending several weeks on shipboard with Rachel as her companion:

> Women of her own age usually boring her, she supposed that girls would be worse. She glanced at Rachel again. Yes! how clear it was that she would be vacillating, emotional, and when you said something to her it would make no more lasting impression than the stroke of a stick upon water. There was nothing to take hold of in girls—nothing hard, permanent, satisfactory [p. 20].

When Rachel announces that she is going on deck "to triumph in the wind," Mrs. Ambrose's worst fears of her niece's romanticism are confirmed. Anticipating their enforced companionship, she walks down the ship's corridor muttering, "Damn, damn, damn." Her character is so strongly and so attractively developed in the early chapters that she, and not Rachel, captures the reader's interest and admiration.

Though Rachel's gaucheries are shown to be the brave risks of naive candor, they are made to seem more ridiculous than pitiable. The author seems to struggle with contempt for her own youthful vulnerability. The force of the narrator's emotion is directed against Rachel's professors and masters who have failed to impart to her "the most elementary idea of a system in modern life" (p. 34). Rachel seeks to know "life" coolly, through books, conversation, and the curious observation of others; she is frightened and sickened by glimpses of fleshly physicality. Indignation rather than sympathy, irony rather than empathy, and the fear of sexual love rather than the longing for it create the emotional climate of the novel.

Virginia Stephen's attitude toward herself, at one moment boldly asserting her rights and her talent, and the next, trembling with humiliation at the sense of her own deficiencies, is temperamental but also understandably conditioned by her position as a young woman artist in a group of well-educated, confident, critical male friends and competitors. This novel, her only major work to be shown to anyone during the period of its composition, was the fruit of great insecurity. Her attitude toward Rachel is understandably ambivalent, for she does not want to offer her as a female scapegoat for male criticism. She is far

more sure of herself with Terence, the alter ego of Rachel. He is the
single exception to a group of male characters in the novel who, as Clive
Bell rather extravagantly commented, seemed to him uniformly "ob-
tuse, vulgar, blind, florid, rude, tactless, emphatic, indelicate, vain,
tyrannical, and stupid."[17]

Revisions made in the interest of controlling emotion can be studied
only by examining late versions in typescript, typed by the author. She
burned seven early versions. The comparison of typescripts with the
published version shows a variety of editing practices, all of which
affect the emotional tone. By aesthetic distancing through style and
point of view as well as by the deliberately restrained use of personal
experience, the young Virginia Stephen attempted to create genuine
but carefully muted emotion.

Her stylistic revisions are often the recasting of sentences for greater
felicity or for epigrammatic succinctness. These changes result in
greater formality and hence accomplish distancing. Her later style was
designed to follow the mind's wanderings and was more various and
flexible. The range of sentence length is greater in the novels after
Jacob's Room. Characteristics are an increase in phrasal and clausal
beginnings, deliberate blockings of thought by digressive elements,
awkwardly detached participles, indefinite pronominal references, deliberate violation of coherence, and dislocation of modifiers. Sentences
often begin and end in a fog of indefiniteness, yet finally achieve clar-
ity.[18] Literary and rhetorical niceties are foregone for the sake of
creating groping sentences that imitate the action of thought. In *The
Voyage Out* revisions, efforts are made to emulate the dying falls of the
conscious stylist, resulting in less identification with the thought of the
characters.

Another type of change is deletion of banal and sentimental expres-
sions of feeling, mostly from the dialogue. Such lover's proclamations
as "There'll be nothing too difficult for us in the whole world so long as
we have each other" are removed. Typical of such clichés, cut in the
final version to a few broken phrases, is the following speech of
Terence, admirably suited for the women's magazine fiction of the
period: "It's over now, the waiting, playing about, observing—all that's
been so unsatisfactory, all the things I've had to pretend, all I've had to
put up with in default of better—I shan't waste time on them again.

Half my life I've wasted—worse than wasted."[19] These changes move in the direction of the novel of Silence, that novel about the things people do not say, which Terence wants to write, the novel that Virginia Woolf did write.

These deletions improve the novel, but there are others that detract from its power to engage the reader in Rachel's plight. The most telling are those passages that refer to Rachel's relationship with her dead mother; they are genuinely moving and might well have increased sympathy for the protagonist. But to arouse compassion publicly for Rachel's orphaned state might have seemed to Virginia Woolf "obviously not good manners." It might also have dangerously touched the deep springs of her own grief for the mother who died suddenly when Virginia Stephen was thirteen. Although she dealt triumphantly with these memories in *To the Lighthouse,* their inclusion in *The Voyage Out* was perhaps not possible for her. Leonard Woolf writes of the threat of such memories: "If when she was well, any situation or argument arose which was closely connected with her breakdowns or the causes of them, there would sometimes rise to the surface of her mind traces or echoes of the nightmares and delusions of her madness, so that it seemed as if deep down in her mind she was never completely sane."[20] Speculations aside, the facts are that the omissions from her typescripts include a number of references to the mother's power over Rachel's life, to Rachel's sense of her mother's mystery, and to her deep-seated longing for her. "Theresa, the dead woman, again made herself felt," reads one deleted line. And the following deleted sentence might be the text for the last section of *To the Lighthouse:* "Nothing is stronger than the position of the dead among the living, and the whole scene was the work of one woman who has been in her grave for eight years." The most significant omission occurs in the earlier version at the moment Terence proposes to Rachel: " 'O Terence,' she cried suddenly, 'The dead. My mother is dead.' "[21] Such an orphaned cry, revealing both the depth of secret sorrow and the fear of sexual love, is poignant. But it was removed from the final version. Only when she had emotionally mastered the experience of her mother's death was she able to use it in her fiction and to infuse it with feeling. And even then there is obvious aesthetic control. Mrs. Ramsay's death is told in a parenthesis. Lily's grief for her is the medium by which the event is felt.

To further control personal emotion in *The Voyage Out,* the mother role is transferred almost entirely to the living presence of an aunt whose mature wisdom is cool. Many physical and personal traits of Mrs. Ramsay (and Julia Stephen and Vanessa Bell, as well) appear in Helen Ambrose. But in spite of the opening scene in which she weeps for her children left behind in her London home, Helen is an amused, permissive, and ironic guide for Rachel rather than a maternal cherisher.

Another experience of personal grief in Virginia Woolf's life seems to be even more relevant to the emotional effect of the novel than the death of Julia Stephen. Two years after that loss, Virginia's older half-sister, Stella Duckworth, died of peritonitis during the first year of her marriage. Stella had deferred her marriage plans to preside over the motherless household, and her bridal happiness was particularly well-deserved. The loss was a sad and shocking one. In October 1940, writing of her memories of this time, Virginia Woolf described the effect of this death on her fifteen-year-old self:

> Again, whether 15 or not, whether [illegible] or not, I must have felt something very acute; merely from the pressure of circumstances. My mother's death had been a latent sorrow—how at 13 would one feel it fully? But Stella's death two years later had a different importance, striking that extraordinarily unshielded yet apprehensive fabric of which the mind and body are made at 15. And yet behind the surface lay the other vision. Even if I were not fully conscious of what my mother's death meant, I had been for two years continually absorbing it. . . . all those negative results . . . the glooms, the morbid [illegible] the shut bedrooms, the giving up of St. Ives, the black clothes, my father's [illegible]—all this had formed my mind and made it apprehensive, made it, I suppose unnaturally responsive to Stella's happiness and the promise it held out for her—when on a moment—unbelievably, catastrophically, I remember saying the impossible has happened and it was unnatural, against the law, horrible, a treachery, a betrayal—and the fact of death, the blow, the second blow of death struck on me, tremulous as a moth from a broken chrysalis.[22]

A like sense of horror at the sudden death of a young woman on the threshold of marriage is meant to be one of the emotional high points of the novel. But it is considerably undercut because the novel's view of marriage and of "life itself" does not promise its heroine happiness. Fearing and doubting, Rachel and Terence thought: "They were impotent; they could never love each other sufficiently to overcome all these barriers and they could never be satisfied with less" (p. 303). The emotional effect is muted—one of metaphysical melancholy rather than of tragic grief.

In addition to the constant revisions made in the interest of genuine but controlled emotion, the typescripts show that Virginia Woolf worked diligently to construct a unified formal pattern for an action that was inconclusive. Therefore the closing paragraph of Lytton Strachey's letter of hyperbolic praise for *The Voyage Out* must have been a body blow. He suggested that "it perhaps lacked the cohesion of a dominating idea—I don't mean in the spirit—but in the action."[23] Her reply was meek and points the way to the highly detailed 508-page *Night and Day:*

> I suspect your criticism about the failure of conception is quite right. I think I had a conception, but I don't think it made itself felt. What I wanted to do was to give the feeling of a vast tumult of life, as various and disorderly as possible, which should be cut short for a moment by the death, and go on again—and the whole was to have a sort of pattern and be somehow controlled. The difficulty was to keep any sort of coherence—also to give enough detail to make the characters interesting—which Forster says I didn't do. I really wanted three volumes. Do you think it's possible to get this sort of effect in a novel; is the result bound to be too scattered to be intelligible? I expect one may learn to get more control in time. One gets much too involved in detail.[24]

To explore the efficacy of three volumes, Virginia Woolf wrote *Night and Day*. It was clearly, and quite deliberately, an effort to go against her own psychological and artistic grain, to keep the dangerous ghosts that had risen in the writing of *The Voyage Out* at bay. She worked out a double plot of search, on the mundane level of London social life, the workings of the feminist movement, and the tentative romantic explorations of five characters. Leonard Woolf explains that she was doing it as a kind of classical exercise. Her own backward look in 1933 when she was working on *The Years,* another "novel of fact," confirms this

view that writing it was a useful experience: "I can take liberties with
the representational form which I could not dare when I wrote *Night
and Day*—a book that taught me much, bad though it may be."[25] But
her diary entries the year of publication (1919) indicate that at the
time she held a higher opinion of its worth: "In my own opinion, *N. &
D.* is a much more mature and finished and satisfactory book than *The
Voyage Out;* as it has reason to be."[26] Thematically, it is more affirmative; the view of marriage, again a central question, is doubting rather
than morbidly fearful. But, on the whole, it is not a success. Certainly,
a social comedy that ends in an engagement is not the best form for her
perspective that life is a mysterious flux and that societal order is an
enemy of the individual order.

A brief examination of the relationship between plot and structure,
the point of view, the style and the characteristic use of image will
suffice to place it in the pattern of her technical search for balance.
Night and Day represents Virginia Woolf's effort to explore the resources of conclusive plot as dominant form. Its realistic documenta-
tion proved incompatible with her perspective, but her mastery of the
pedestrian fictional techniques of moving characters in space and time,
arranging their confrontations, and balancing the advance of two plot
lines later gave strength to her major novels. In *Mrs. Dalloway* the
reader is made aware of the forward movement of the action at all
times, in spite of the fluid use of time.

The plot of *Night and Day* is the search of its main characters, four
young Londoners, and a minor character, a country cousin, for a mean
between the day life of obligation and social exchange and the night life
of solitude and dreams. In love and work they hope to find freedom
and wholeness. The possibility of communication still seems woefully
dim and the illusions of romantic longings becloud understanding, but
the outlook is more positive than the dark view of *The Voyage Out* that
life is in all probability a fruitless search for meaning. The outer action
is not in perfect harmony with the uneasy questioning beneath the
surface, however, and the details of everyday life are tedious and
lengthy; the characters' ruminations and hesitations make them ineffec-
tual wanderers in the quotidian world. There is a more serious fault—
the reader is rarely moved.

The structure of the novel is the almost mechanical contrast of
alternating episodes: inner, silent explorations and outer, inconclusive

dialogues between major characters. This logically parallels the central action and is harmonious with the perspective but lacks the variety and complexity of movement characteristic of her later fiction.

The symbols used throughout are natural—for example, the Hilberry home radiates stable cultural values, sending out into the dark streets the light of wisdom, peace, and joy. Even when the symbols are dual, their evocations are less richly developed than those found in her later work.

In *The Voyage Out,* Virginia Woolf established her characteristic perspective and her characteristic pattern of action, but failed to command the technical and emotional power to fuse them. In *Night and Day,* she tried to achieve unity and coherence by a more detailed realism, a method she had scorned. She did not abandon her perspective or the quest plot, but the poetic truths behind them, when baldly presented by authorial assertion, seem banalities. Although *Night and Day* has many subtle representations of thought and feeling, it too often falls into such flat statements as this description of Katherine Hilberry's mental life:

> To seek a true feeling among the chaos of the unfeelings or the half-feelings of life, to recognize it when found and to accept the consequences of the discovery, draws lines upon the smoothest brow, while it quickens the light of the eyes; it is a pursuit which alternately is bewildering, debasing, and exalting, and as Katherine speedily found, her discoveries gave her equal cause for surprise, shame, and intense anxiety.[27]

To compare this passage with the opening pages of *Mrs. Dalloway* in which feelings, unfeelings, and half-feelings are dramatized rather than generalized upon is to see why, having improved her skill at plotting outer action, Virginia Woolf continued her search for balance between the inner and the outer by attempting a more immediate rendering of mental life.

chapter Six

Freedom and form: *Jacob's Room*

In the opening scene of The Voyage Out, *Helen Ambrose* stands on the Waterloo Bridge embankment, weeping and gazing into the Thames. The narrator describes the view:

> Sometimes the flats and churches and hotels of Westminster are like the outlines of Constantinople in the mist: sometimes the river is an opulent purple, sometimes mud-colored, sometimes sparkling blue like the sea. It is always worth while to look down and see what is happening. But this lady looked neither up nor down; the only thing she had seen, since she stood there, was a circular irides- cent patch slowly floating past and with a straw in the middle of it. The straw and patch swam again and again behind the tremulous medium of a great welling tear, and the tear rose and fell and dropped into the river [p. 10].

The second paragraph of *Jacob's Room* also describes a weeping woman by the water. Betty Flanders writes a letter at the seaside:

Slowly welling from the point of her gold nib, pale blue ink dissolved the full stop; for there her pen stuck; her eyes fixed, and tears slowly filled them. The entire bay quivered; the lighthouse wobbled; and she had the illusion that the mast of Mr. Connor's little yacht was bending like a wax candle in the sun. She winked quickly. Accidents were awful things. She winked again. The mast was straight; the waves were regular; the lighthouse was upright; but the blot had spread [p. 7].

In both passages the imagery is designed to link subject and object, the exterior scene and the emotional experiences of the character. But in the second there are significant differences in the point of view, psychological complexity, and emotional effect. The identity of the welling ink and the welling tear, the less literary physical description, the informality of syntax, the seemingly dissociated interpolation, and the liveliness of the mental action all greatly sophisticate the imaginative act required of the reader. The narrator as literary commentator has disappeared; the imitation of consciousness is more immediate and more intense.

Even this limited comparison of narrative technique is enough to show why all readers rightly see in *Jacob's Room* an exciting mutation of her method that would lead to the realization of her major work. Those whose opinion she respected praised her privately, and the press was kind, but later critics of the whole body of her work find *Jacob's Room* overshadowed by the mature works that followed. She herself was, as always, sharply critical of her own accomplishment.

The most common charge against the novel is that her newly acquired freedom to imitate random experience, to give "the sense of life," is not effectively matched by her power to create an emotional "sense of conclusiveness." Yet the failure was not caused by inattention to the problem; her plans for *Jacob's Room* began by stating the question: "I think the main point is that it should be free. But what about form?"[1] She did achieve the freedom; she did create an aesthetic form. Why did their interplay fail to produce the strong emotional power she believed critical to the success of fiction?

The plot of *Jacob's Room* is a search for the means to understand one life—that of a young man whose varied but undramatic experiences are cut off by an early death. He is Jacob Flanders, less an individual than an archetypal figure, vaguely "distinguished," "obscure," and "monolithic" (pp. 70, 164). Although valued by both men and women, he is never deeply engaged with another person; conversations are not so much dialogues as snatches of talk. Because one aspect of the novel's perspective is "that a profound impartial, and absolutely just opinion of our fellow-creatures is utterly unknown" (p. 71), these epithets and his relationships are not fully explored. Always inferring tentatively, the narrator commonly views Jacob from the outside, recording the details of his milieu and of his friends' reactions to him, sometimes his fleeting sensory impressions or a stray thought, but only rarely his decisions, analyses, or evaluations. *Jacob's Room* is the ambience of Jacob's experience, not the intimate chamber of his mind.[2]

The narrator and reader jointly search for his life's meaning; this novel is not the quest of Jacob Flanders himself. " 'What for? What for?' Jacob never asked himself any such questions, to judge by the way he laced his boots; shaved himself; to judge by the depth of his sleep that night, with the wind fidgeting at the shutters, and half-a-dozen mosquitoes singing in his ears" (p. 161). It is, then, the vibrant consciousness of the narrator, a self-styled observer, that experiences the frissons of mortality, the visions of "people passing tragically to destruction" that evoke "a curious sadness, as if time and eternity showed through skirts and waistcoats" (p. 168).

The theme denies the possibility of knowing character, but the art celebrates the moments of vitality that constitute Jacob's experience. The reader senses intuitively that the value of this life lies in the degree of its awareness, the quality of its response to beauty and intelligence. After Jacob's death, the movement of the wind in the curtains and the creaking of Jacob's empty chair hint that the dead man is now part of the "life itself" that is the book's affirmative center. The power of *Jacob's Room* lies in the intensity and freedom with which it imitates this life. But the novel's form implies no certainty in event; it remains open and contingent, yet attempts to offer the compensation of the harmonious order of art. Ultimately the reader must sense order through the patterning of the seemingly miscellaneous details.

With a keen sense of adventuring Virginia Woolf worked out the technical changes that accomplish these effects in a series of sketches and short stories written between 1917 and 1921. In "The Mark on the

Wall," "Kew Gardens," and "An Unwritten Novel" she experimented with new ways of achieving her old goal of balance between freedom and form. The first and third of these stories developed the plot of inconclusive, associative mental quest, and "Kew Gardens" developed the structure of alternation which was to stabilize the loose narrative.

The essaylike "The Mark on the Wall" (1917) is the musing of a speaker who idly tries to identify, without actual inspection, the nature of a dark spot on the fireplace wall. The slight search plot ends amusingly and abruptly when a more literal-minded visitor enters and observes that the mark is a snail. The interest of the piece obviously lies not in that limiting identification but in the richness of the fantasy in which the speaker proposes for the spot a variety of possible identities and in passing ruminates on, among other things, Shakespeare, Victorian tablecloths, and antiquarians.

The source of her inspiration for such imaginative associational form has aroused critical speculation. E. M. Forster, comparing passages from both *Tristram Shandy* and *The Mark on the Wall,* shows their authors' affinities. And Virginia Woolf herself expressed admiration for the form of *Tristram Shandy* because it "seems to allow the writer to put down at once the first thought that comes into his head."[3] Other critics assume more contemporary influence and to them Leonard Woolf speaks in *Downhill All the Way,* after questioning the validity of the concept of "influence." He notes that while there are those who assert "Virginia derived her method, which they call the stream of consciousness, from Joyce and Dorothy Richardson . . . it is perhaps just worth while to point out that *The Mark on the Wall* had been written at latest in the first part of 1917, while it was not until April, 1918, that Virginia read *Ulysses* in manuscript and January, 1919, that she read *The Tunnel.*"[4]

Her work was in the stream of a new literary convention being contemporaneously evolved in poetry and fiction; it is compatible with contemporary psychology and philosophy; she was by her own records aware of the work of other novelists engaged in similar technical experiments. One is inclined to protest at first that Leonard Woolf is excessively touchy on this question. Yet a temperament so passionately resentful of authority or intrusion, so consecrated to the realization of her private vision, so intuitively jealous of the writer's freedom and independence, is more likely to be dismayed by another writer's likeness than to profit by his discoveries. Reading Proust with reluctant and almost resentful admiration, she writes: "He will, I suppose, both influence me and make me out of temper with every sentence of my own."[5] In a letter to Roger Fry she says of reading *Swann's Way:* "Oh, if I could write like that! I try. And at the moment such is the astonishing vibration and saturation and intensification that he procures—there's something sexual in it—that I feel I *can* write like that, and seize my pen and then I *can't* write like that. Scarcely anyone so stimulates the nerves of language in me; it becomes an obsession."[6]

In contrast to this spontaneous response to a writer so close to her own creative imagination, Virginia Woolf's characteristic reaction to the work of another writer imitating mental life was to analyze the *effect* of his work with great care, and if it pleased her, to work out her own method of arriving at it. In her 1917 review of Dostoevsky's *The Eternal Husband,* she praised his power of reconstructing conscious thought as well as of suggesting "the dim and populous underworld of the mind's consciousness where desires and impulses are moving blindly beneath the sod."[7] But in the paragraph preceding this tribute is her own metaphor for this action which confirms her recognition of Dostoevsky's artistry:

> As we ourselves are conscious of thinking when some startling fact has dropped into the pool of our consciousness: from the crowd of objects pressing upon our attention we select now this one, now that one, weaving them inconsequently into our thought; the associations of a word perhaps make another loop in the line from which we spring back again to a different section of our main thought, and the whole process seems both inevitable and perfectly lucid. But if we try to reconstruct our mental processes later, we find that the links between one thought and another are submerged. The chain is sunk out of sight and only the leading points emerge to mark the course.[8]

She is here following her *own* method, not Dostoevsky's, and though over a period of two years (1921-1923) she collaborated with S. S. Koteliansky on translations of Dostoevsky for the Hogarth Press, she preserved her independence by defining with the most delicate discrimination the distinctions between her goals and methods and those of the Russian she admired.

In any case, what most distinguishes her imitation of mental experience from that of others also using the technique of association is the wealth of its imagery. For this she needed no literary model. Thought that is imagistic, synesthetic, animistic, and nontemporal is "primary process thinking," which medical texts describe as common to disturbed mental states such as those she painfully experienced.[9] Her serious illnesses were prolonged suicidal nightmares, as Leonard Woolf testifies. Her mild illnesses sometimes meant weeks of torpor, racing thoughts, and pain, but she made courageous use of these as a writer, calling them "curious intervals in life"; "I've had many," she wrote in her diary, "most fruitful artistically—one becomes fertilised—think of my madness at Hogarth—and all the little illnesses—that before I wrote the *Lighthouse* for instance."[10]

To write a full-length novel of epistemological search making the richest use of her supernormal imagination, she sought a subject. And the 1921 sketch, "An Unwritten Novel," evolved the plot model for *Jacob's Room:* the narrator imagines the life story of a woman sitting opposite in a railway carriage. In this scenario, invented by the inductive reasoning of a curious, sympathetic, imaginative stranger, the woman emerges as an unhappy, guilt-ridden spinster. But the narrator's Freudian guessing is proved false when her fellow passenger, alighting, is met by her son. Undaunted, the narrator continues her quest for the understanding of the elusive human personality, calling after them: "Mysterious figures! Who are you?" With similar self-conscious rhetoric the narrator breaks in on the imagistic descriptions of the world of Jacob Flanders.

In the 1920 experimental sketch, "Kew Gardens," the montage structure of *Jacob's Room* was developed. The narrator describes a July afternoon in the London public gardens on three levels of experience: the world of plants, birds, and a snail (a world in which all colors and movements are intensified and magnified); the world of the audible and desultory conversations between pairs of strollers; and the worlds of their silent musings and memories. "Kew Gardens" is composed of description, fragmented conversations, and inner monologues; the latter are either evocative memories or anticipatory visions called up by the objects in the garden. (Similar fleeting glimpses of the lives and pasts of passersby create much of the background in both *Jacob's Room* and *Mrs. Dalloway.*) The strollers see and remember. The method generalizes character; the speakers are as universal as the person behind the lyric poem.

This sketch marks Virginia Woolf's fuller use of the technique of selecting and fusing visual details that in *Jacob's Room* successfully sharpens experience and imitates the transience of the living world. Its evanescent visual imagery is in constant flux, dissolving and reforming patterns; the narrator's account follows the selective and sometimes distorting movements of the human eye and brain, both apprehending and merging its flowing details: "Yellow and black, pink and snow white, shapes of all these colours, men, women, and children were spotted for a second upon the horizon, and then, seeing the breadth of yellow that lay upon the grass, they wavered and sought shade beneath the trees, dissolving like drops of water in the yellow and green atmosphere, staining it faintly with red and blue" (p. 34).

Here the eye of the writer behaves like the eye of a painter. In fact, Jean Guiguet speculates that the idea for the sketch may have arisen from Virginia Woolf's review of Arnold Bennett's *Books and Persons* (*TLS*, July 5, 1917) in which she quotes approvingly Bennett's own question from his essay "Neo-Impressionism and Literature": "Is it not possible that some writer will come along and do in words what these men have done in paint?"[11] But such a provocative question is only the beginning of a difficult search for means. To change representation and design from a medium in which visual details are composed in space to a medium in which they are arranged in time is a radical translation.

At this period she was exploring the relationships between painting and writing with special excitement. Writing to Vanessa Bell in 1918, she promises to send what seems to be the unpublished "Kew Gardens." Calling it "a case of atmosphere," she wonders whether she as "got it right," and goes on in the same paragraph, as if by association, to say: "I'm going to write an account of my emotions towards one of your pictures which gives me infinite pleasure and has changed my views on aesthetics. . . . All this is very complicated and I must write a special letter about it. It's a question of half-developed aesthetic emotions constantly checked by others of a literary nature."[12] Notebook entries about the same date are somewhat incoherent and illegible comments on Vanessa's painting, which she describes as works of severe design and logical beauty, suffused with color, warmth, and life. Her own conscious effort to achieve the same balance seems plain.

The relationship between Vanessa Bell's painting and Virginia Woolf's writing is brilliantly discussed by Richard Morphet in "The Art of Vanessa Bell," the introduction to the catalog of the December, 1973 London exhibition of her work:

> There is a parallel between this passionate looking and noting and her sister's writing. The way one object leans upon another, the reality of cups, of a book that has just been put down, the mysterious life of a piece of furniture that has existed in another age—these kinds of awareness seem to be expressed in her work. . . . In the paintings of Vanessa Bell's last four decades, particularly in her still-lifes, one can really feel her excitement in the sheer felicity and variety of form and colour there to be appreciated in objects however mundane,—and in their juxtapositions.

Indeed it is very difficult to decide out of context whether the following sentence of Mr. Morphet's, describing Vanessa Bell's painting, refers to the prose of Virginia or to the canvasses of Vanessa: "The communication of the living reality of a brief time-span of perception of nature in all its felt freshness is fitted with complete naturalness into (or made to create) the same kind of limpid structure with which she was concerned in her early work."

By a reasonable analogy Winifred Holtby described the fictional technique that resulted from Virginia Woolf's experimentation in the direction of Vanessa's painting as "cinematic" and implied the influence of the film; Virginia Woolf, however, in a personal letter called Miss Holtby's book "wildly inaccurate." Virginia Woolf was imitating not the cinema but her own hypersensitive visual processes, accompanied by continual questioning and evaluation and emotional uneasiness. But the technique that emerged—in effect dynamic montage—can be fruitfully described in the language of cinematography. In fact, Sergei Eisenstein, writing eight years after the publication of *Jacob's Room,* in one of the earliest discussions of the aesthetics of the film, uses terminology perfectly suited to the technical analysis of that novel: distortion, stop-motion and slow motion, visual angle, close and long shots, conflicts between an event and its duration, framed details, and emotional effects of transition and disintegration. In his afterword to N. Kaufman's pamphlet *Japanese Cinema* (1929), he uses a literary form, the haiku, to illustrate his central concept of the montage, "a maximum laconism for the visual representation of abstract concepts."[13] The notebook plan for the "Time Passes" section of *To the Lighthouse* is a series of unpolished haiku and tonka, concrete in detail, abstract in suggestion:

> The Seasons
> The Skull
> The gradual dissolution of everything
>
> Sun, moon, stars
> Hopeless gulfs of misery
>
> Shawls and shooting capes
> The devouringness of nature
> But all this frames, accumulates
> Darkness
> The welling wind and water[14]

Of course the phenomenological assumptions underlying much art of this period—the poetry of Pound, Stevens, and Eliot—resulted in similar techniques. Their poetry, like the film, combined "shots that are depictive, single in meaning, and neutral in content into intellectual contexts and series."[15] And the method is based on psychological and social assumptions as well. Eisenstein writes: "Absolute reality is by no means the correct form of perception. It is simply the function of a certain form of social structure. . . . By combining . . . incongruities we newly collect the disintegrated event into one whole but in *our* aspect."[16] Virginia Woolf's insistence that the writer must find means to realize his private vision and that through art he resists the paralyzing influence of society is perfectly in agreement. It is logical that she should have developed a fictional method that is harmonious with these techniques. Yet she was certainly working on independent lines, attempting to unify the plot of search and the structure of montage that she had developed in these three short pieces.

Her diary shows that in *Jacob's Room,* she consciously fused the techniques of all three sketches hoping to realize throughout a full-length novel the movement, the selectivity, the immediacy, the intensity, and the associative search of a consciousness looking for meaning, abandoning predictable, conventionally established narrative pattern.[17] In fact, *Jacob's Room* is almost entirely controlled by aesthetic principles found in the theories of Roger Fry and Charles Mauron; its structure is formed by contrasts of visual and emotional experience rhythmically repeated—in Fry's critical vocabulary—"plastic" rather than narrative values. In *Jacob's Room* she gives the world as spectacle.

To a high degree her technical goals were achieved. In *Jacob's Room* she did imitate the free movement of the mind, the eye, and the feelings through a flexible syntax, bold leaps of association, the juxtaposition of brilliant images, and visual analogues for emotion. Long, complex, but easily grasped sentences successfully follow the windings of reverie:

> "Oh, bother Mr. Floyd!" said Jacob switching off a thistle's head, for he knew already that Mr. Floyd was going to teach them Latin, as indeed he did for three years in his spare time, out of kindness, for there was no other gentleman in the neighborhood whom Mrs. Flanders could have asked to do such a thing, and the elder boys were getting beyond her, and must be got ready for school, and it was more than most clergymen would have done, coming round after tea, or having them in his own room—as he could fit it in—for the parish was a very large one, and Mr. Floyd, like his father before him, visited cottages miles away on the moors, and, like old Mr. Floyd, was a great scholar, which made it so unlikely—she had never dreamt of such a thing [p. 20].

Such shifts—from Jacob's speech to Betty Flanders' thoughts, from the present moment to a glimpse into the future to a reverie in that future becomes present-all within a single sentence, are paralleled by frequent shifts in the angle of vision. In one passage, a drowsing child is seen through the eyes of the narrator, but in mid-paragraph the view becomes what is seen through the child's half-closed eyes.

To sharpen detail and to compress description, she makes use of the eye's propensity to pick out and to linger on striking images:

As the wood caught, the city of London was lit up for a second; on other sides of the fire there were trees. Of the faces which came out fresh and vivid as though painted in yellow and red, the most prominent was a girl's face. By a trick of the firelight she seemed to have no body. The oval of the face and hair hung beside the fire with a dark vacuum for background. As if dazed by the glare, her green-blue eyes stared at the flames [p. 74].

This is the painter's and the photographer's trick of highlighting; it allows freedom and economy in representation and heightens emotion. In *Jacob's Room* many such images exist for the excitement they convey; sometimes they are repeated in changing form for special meaning.

Expressionistic imagery is brilliantly used. In one scene, Jacob Flanders stands in the glare of the streetlamp, shattered by jealousy after seeing his light love, Florinda, with another man: "It was as if a stone were ground to dust; as if white sparks flew from a livid whetstone, which was his spine; as if the switchback railway, having swooped to the depths, fell, fell, fell. This was in his face" (p. 94).

This fluid recreation of heterogeneous physical and emotional experiences achieved that "main point"—that *Jacob's Room* should be "free." The question "But what about form?" was answered in a way that was consistent with the organizing principle of a search for balance between order and disorder. It was a marked change from the form of *Night and Day*. She abandoned the perspective that shapes that novel— the belief that balanced reconciliation of the outer and the inner lives may be arrived at through acts of will that bring about briefly satisfying human relationships. *Jacob's Room* returns to the perspective of the less hopeful *The Voyage Out*—that human experience is essentially lonely and inexplicable and perhaps only in full communion with others after death. Unlike that of both the earlier novels, the form of *Jacob's Room* is not determined by a struggle between opposite forces with ambivalent values. *Jacob's Room* is a world in which the unreconciled coexistence of order and disorder is not deeply questioned; the social criticism of the earlier novels is greatly muted. Perhaps this is why, although as Carolyn Heilbrun notes, *Jacob's Room* is a war novel, making plain the human waste of conflict, it is rarely honored as one.[18] It is a world of alternating contrasts rather than one of conflicts leading to a fusion of polarities. Its structure is alternation; "intensity of life to be compared with immobility." Its balance is attained without tension and conflict; death does not conquer "the unseizable force" of life.

Given this inconclusive plot, Virginia Woolf built a strong structure to create the aesthetic whole that her theory of the novel required. Although she did not systematize or work by rigid plan, a macrostructure can be discerned, formed by three principles of contrast which are conceptual. There is a microstructure as well; it is formed by recurring patterns of images, that repetition with variety which Forster calls "rhythm." The major divisions of the novel's progress are milieus that are symbols of order: Jacob's childhood home, Cambridge, the British Museum, St. Paul's, his London apartment, and all gatherings of friendship, gaiety, beauty, harmony, and intellectual interchange. Around these flows the disordered vitality of nature and of common life.

In addition to the mindlessness of the natural world, another kind of disorder threads through Jacob's life—his private rebellions and his occasional resistance to social categorization. "There is something absolute in us which despises qualification," says the narrator. "It is that which is teased and twisted in society" (p. 144). Jacob's resistance takes the form of illicit sexual encounters, antisocial withdrawals, experiences of inexplicable loneliness and melancholy. Yet life's forms and freedoms are not pitted desperately against each other as they are in the earlier novels. Jacob, as a man, is not threatened by the male-created systems of authority as is Rachel Vinrace, and as a student, he is not confined by the demands of a profession or by home responsibilities as is Ralph Denham in *Night and Day*. Teased and twisted by society, his identity is supported nonetheless by social values and institutions. All contrasts of experience alternate without affecting his freedom of choice; the world winks at his rebellions.

On the other hand, the women to whom Jacob is attracted are victims of the social order. Among them is Clara Durrant, the proper young girl of good family, "a virgin chained to a rock (somewhere off Lowndes Square) eternally pouring out tea for old men in white waistcoats" (p. 123). And the little artist's model, Fanny Elmer, discovering herself pregnant, is "caught by the heel" (p. 168).

Recurring major principles emerge from the contrasts of episodes and backgrounds: order and disorder, the past and the present, and stasis and movement. All are at work in the scenes at Cambridge where

Jacob experiences "a sense of old buildings and time, himself the inheritor" (p. 45) and simultaneously participates in scenes teeming with current life.

The rhythmic alternation of nearly static scenes with representations of action is emphasized by the visual technique of spacing between vignettes. And the method has several uses: it makes possible many broad leaps in time as well as the timeless extension of visionary moments. Virginia Woolf defines the technique in describing the method of Sterne: "an alteration in the movement of the mind which makes it pause and widen its gaze and slightly change its attention. We are looking out at life in general." [19] Consciously or intuitively, she uses it to establish a subtle, subliminally experienced rhythm of stop-and-go that balances the discontinuous and uneven chronological progress of Jacob's story. This passage, which reads like Sergei Eisenstein's "shot lists" for his cameramen, catches in brief the tempo:

> A window tinged yellow about two feet across alone combated the white fields and the black trees. . . . At six o'clock a man's figure carrying a lantern crossed the field. . . . A raft of twigs stayed upon a stone, suddenly detached itself, and floated towards the culvert. . . . A load of snow slipped and fell from a fir branch. . . . Later there was a mournful cry. . . . A motor car came along the road shoving the dark before it. . . . The dark shut down behind it.
>
> Spaces of complete immobility separated each of these movements. [Pp. 98-99]

The hint of death in the midst of life is here.

Contrasts of time, values, and movement appear in the alternating sequence of narrative, descriptive, and dramatic passages; sometimes all three contrasts are simultaneously made. The Parthenon stands above the tumultuous, dirty, ugly life of the streets of Athens, juxtaposing past and present, the enduring and the ephemeral, stasis and flux. Repeated images take on incremental significance. Images from the first chapter, objects that appear in minor incidents in Jacob's childhood, recur throughout the novel. Brief actions are repeated. Jacob's brother Archer calls him at the seashore, the sound of his voice evoking lonely futility and isolation. In the final scene his friend calls: " 'Jacob! Jacob!' cried Bonamy, standing by the window. The leaves sank down again" (p. 176). Similarly in the one-page closing chapter, an understated revelation of Jacob's death in war, appear three clusters of images from earlier episodes; all at this moment acquire a richer meaning. The reader able to summon up their context experiences simultaneously a sharp sense of the continuity and mutability of existence. But the images characterize Jacob's rooms, not his essence; they offer no clues to the quester.

What are the flaws of this "new form" in terms of Virginia Woolf's own theory of the novel? Her *TLS* review, "A Glance at Turgenev," which appeared the year *Jacob's Room* was published (1921), shows that at this time she still believed that an episodic action, strengthened by a structure of contrast and infused with universalized emotions, could succeed as a persuasive fictional form. Praising Turgenev's *The Two Friends* for succeeding in realizing it, she writes:

> Thus the first scene which was so lively and suggestive has led to other scenes; they add themselves to it; they bring in contrast, distance, solidity. In the end everything seems to be there. Here is a world able to exist by itself. Now perhaps we can talk with some certainty of a master; for now we have not a single brilliant episode which is gone the moment after, but a succession of scenes attached to one another by the feelings which are common to humanity.[20]

Jacob's Room has just such continuity, just such design, but it fails to generate expectation or sustained emotion. Rather, the emotion flows from the diffused angst of the narrator expressing her melancholy belief that "loveliness is infernally sad" (p. 49). The points of interest are meant to be the narrator's interpolations of "the common feelings of humanity," but these intrusions are ineffective, not because authorial intrusion is damaging per se, but because it points up a fundamental discrepancy in the point of view which, if left unremarked by the narrator, might have succeeded artistically. They are sometimes self-pitying, as well.

The point of view is committed to reporting nothing about Jacob Flanders that the observer cannot know. Consequently, the narrator complains of universal human isolation: " 'Try to penetrate,' for as we lift the cup, shake the hand, express the hope, someone whispers, Is this all? Can I never know, share, be certain?" (p. 93). But the narrator does enter the minds of other characters and profess to generalize about human nature as well, often advancing as universal a response that strikes the reader as idiosyncratic: "Male beauty in association with female beauty breeds in the onlooker a sense of fear" (p. 96). This is not the stock response of all onlookers to the possibility of sexual encounter, as is implied. The intermittent omniscient and limited point of view is inherent in the concept of the novel, but it is clumsy because the narrator calls attention to its inconsistency. She sternly checks herself after describing the outward appearance of Jacob's jealous rage: "Whether we know what was in his mind is another question" (p. 94). In a similar passage she reads his thoughts, then refuses to support the truth of her insight: "But whether this is the right interpretation of Jacob's gloom as he sat naked in the sun, looking at Land's End, it is impossible to say; for he never spoke a word" (p. 49). Even though she exclaims about the impossible task of penetrating the human heart, she brilliantly shows Betty Flanders' mind as she determines to reject the proposal of Mr. Floyd. The narrator's impassioned and sometimes precious lamenting of the impenetrable human mystery seems occasionally illogical and overwrought.

In addition, the novel sometimes suffers from that same emotional imbalance—the failure to strike the mean between too close involvement and too cold a distancing—that damages the emotional unity of *The Voyage Out*. The necessity, inherent in the perspective of *Jacob's Room*, to forego an intimate inner view forbids Jacob the reader's full sympathetic identification. The death of such a shadowy young man, for all his charm, does not arouse the reader's keenest responses. The narrator's obligatory objectivity towards Jacob insists that he cannot be known, but it occasionally falters and lapses; in an elegiac tone at odds with the cool portrayal of the hero, she mourns his inevitable passing. The private emotional experience behind the narrative has broken through; the narrator assumes that she speaks for all. But hers is a personal sorrow and the effect is pathetic, not tragic—digressive, not climactic.

The problems that she posed herself are, as usual, complex. She began the book with a form in mind rather than a subject, as she recorded in her diary. But few read the novel without knowing that

Jacob Flanders is modeled to some extent after her brother, Julian Thoby Stephen, who died in London at the age of twenty-five from typhoid fever contracted on a holiday in Greece. Reading the novel for the first time, Lytton Strachey wrote Virginia Woolf: "Of course, I see something of Thoby in him, as I suppose you intended."[21] And a Strachey letter to an Oxford friend, written while Thoby was living, verifies that resemblance by using some of the rather uncommon adjectives that appear in the novel seventeen years later:

> He has a wonderful and massive frame. His character is as splendid as his appearance, and as wonderfully complete. In fact, he's *monolithic*. But if it were not for his extraordinary sense of humour, he would hardly be of this world. We call him the Goth; and when you see him I'm sure you'll agree that he's a survival of *barbaric* grandeur. He'll be a judge of great eminence, and, in his old age, a sombre family potentate.[22] [Italics added.]

Thoby appears again, of course, as the prototype for the dead hero Percival in *The Waves,* the powerful controlling figure behind the lives of six friends who love him. Upon completing its last chapter, Virginia Woolf wrote movingly: "Anyhow, it's done; and I have been sitting here these 15 minutes in a state of glory, and calm, and some tears, thinking of Thoby and if I could write Julian Thoby Stephen 1881-1906 on the first page. I suppose not."[23]

She had been, as she said, "engaged in anguish" long after his death; the violence and the painful inhibition of grief are present in this entry, even after twenty-five years. Quentin Bell relates that, burdened by the sense that as a younger sister she had not fully known him, she tried to learn more of her dead brother from his friends. They found it impossible to tell her the things she wanted to know.[24] Her creation of Jacob Flanders' Cambridge life and his relations with women were perhaps an effort to bring him closer by imaginatively filling in the blanks. But for the most part in portraying Jacob she holds sternly to the novel's assumption that he cannot be known.

For clear conceptual reasons Jacob Flanders is not a portrait of Thoby Stephen. Virginia Woolf was quite capable of painting a precisely particularized likeness had she wished to do so, as the details of her correspondence with Violet Dickinson immediately following his death show. At that time a bizarre circumstance forced her to transcend her sorrow through her talents as an artist; the necessity was only one of a series of cruel events in 1906 that were particularly painful to her. The four Stephen young people (Vanessa, Thoby, Virginia, and Adrian) were living together at 46 Gordon Square, London, where they had moved after their father's death in 1904. The trip to Greece, together with Violet Dickinson, was high-heartedly undertaken. Vanessa, Violet, and Thoby were all ill as a result; Thoby's death was shattering, especially for Virginia. Two days after Thoby died Vanessa became engaged to Clive Bell, her long-time suitor, and "radiantly happy," left Virginia, courageous but intermittently bitter at the desertion, with Adrian. Since Violet Dickinson was, as Thoby had been, critically ill, Virginia did not have the support of her sympathy.

Advised that news of Thoby's death would worsen Violet's condition, she continued to write her friend almost daily for a month as though Thoby were alive and convalescing. It was a generous deed; Violet's letters had always come in the past, as she had earlier written her, "like balm to the heart," and as she was in need of comfort in what she called a world "like a burnt out moon."[25]

But even under such a strain, she was, as a born writer, able to imagine thoroughly convincing homely details of Thoby's progress back to health; he calls for mutton chops and beer, Nelly brings him carnations, he teases the nurse, Peter reads him Milton, he is reading the reviews of Maitland's life of his father. Writing these letters, she is keeping him alive, and her courage and her pain are moving. At the same time the wit of some statements of double meaning is almost macabre: "Dear old Thoby is still on his back—but manages to be about as full of life in that position as most people are on their hind legs."[26] And five days after his death: "The Dr. says his brain is the strongest he knows and his heart is fit to do the work of two men."[27]

When at last she wrote Violet the truth, she explained her "lies": "The only thing I feel I could not bear would be to think the news should make you worse. I know you loved him and he loved you." The next lines reflect the hero-worship that made the characterization of a young man patterned after Thoby, if only in part, so difficult to control emotionally: "He was so brave and strong and his life was perfect ... Thoby was splendid to the end."[28] Her letters to him at Cambridge reflect this same adulation. Laughingly, but consistently, she calls him "your mightiness" and "your highness," soliciting his judgment on her literary opinions, though she maintains her independence, and envying him his intellectual friendships and opportunities. Although he was only a year older, he assumes avuncular stature.

To avoid too close identification with her own grief and to satisfy the concept of the novel, she used only the traits of Thoby compatible with the character of Jacob as a mystery, omitting specific details that would have made him less archetypal. Thoby's letters to Clive Bell, written in the post-Cambridge days when he was a London law student, reveal many delightful aspects of his personality that do not appear in Jacob: a love of jolly tramping, crabbing, and beagling afternoons, a gift for witty sketching, a talent for the telling phrase, an acute delight in reasoning, a deliberate control of emotion, a confident taste in the arts, and a growing interest in politics, tempered with an amused detachment. Instead of these details Virginia Woolf chose to reflect in other ways the pairs of mildly contradictory qualities that show through them all: his assurance and clumsiness, his dignity and boyishness, his intelligence and lack of introspection, but above all, what all observers noted and admired, the intellectual poise and promise that unified his personality.

As a result of this generalization of character, there is a conflict between the theme of Jacob's unknowability and the climaxes of the novel that insist upon his rare individuality. The moments of the narrator's lamentations are meant to be like those of Turgenev, high points in which reader and speaker share emotions "common to all humanity." Yet they are not deeply powerful because the narrator's feeling is out of proportion to that of the reader. They have not been well prepared for. In "The Two Friends" which she so much admired, Turgenev, by entering the thoughts of a character less humanly promising than Jacob, creates a deeper sense of his meaningless death because he has created a deeper sense of his inner life.

Aware of these questions, she was tormented by her usual retrospective doubts. As always, they were, although exaggerated, essentially sound self-criticism. They formed the rationale for her next attempt at balancing between sentimentality and coldness. She found fault with the form and the tone of *Jacob's Room.* To begin with, she feared the critics would think it "a disconnected rhapsody," believing that the lyrical form was not clearly limned and that the emotional high points were not effective. E. M. Forster, fully acquainted with her theory of the novel as spectral architecture, saw and praised its underlying plan in terms of her own Ruskinian metaphor:

> The coherence of the book is even more amazing than its beauty. In the stream of glittering similes, unfinished sentences, hectic catalogues, unanchored proper names, we seem to be going nowhere. Yet the goal comes, and the method and matter prove to have been one, and looking back from the pathos of the closing scene, we see for a moment the airy drifting of atoms piled into a colonnade.[29]

But she herself was not satisfied with its coherence and wrote to Charles Percy Sanger criticizing the occasional looseness: "I think a close study of *Jacob's Room,* should you ever wish to approach the book again, will reveal many passages which a trained mind would have pinched much closer together. . . ."[30]

The tone was a problem. Forster's word "pathos" was echoed by Lytton Strachey, who in a letter to the author accused her of being "very romantic."[31] From these friends such words may have been euphemisms for "sentimentality," the bête noir of Bloomsbury. Virginia Woolf acknowledged Strachey's criticism promptly with typical apologetics: "I breathe more freely now—Of course you put your infallible finger on the spot—romanticism. How do I catch it? Not from my father. I think it must come from my Great Aunts. But some of it, I think, comes from the effort of breaking with complete representation. One flies into the air. Next time I mean to stick closer to the facts."[32] The breaking with complete representation entailed the time jumps that made room for the authorial intrusions with the egotistical romantic air. Forster congratulated her for having gotten rid of "the sensitive sorrower" as narrator and for having infused the great part of the novel with joy. But "the sensitive sorrower" was indeed occasionally to be heard. Forster believed that such "endorsements" of the characters robbed them of continuous life, and, indeed, that given the perspectives of Virginia Woolf's novels it was impossible to build the vital "permanent roads of love and hate" that must exist between characters.

Both Fry and Forster questioned the validity of presenting life chiefly as a flow of exquisite sensibility. Virginia Woolf perhaps implicitly acknowledged this criticism in *Mrs. Dalloway* by balancing the inner mental action with more dramatic outer action. Fry accused her of "poetizing"—exaggerating the excitement and importance of sensory experience and imposing her own personality.[33] Perhaps anticipating his criticism, she had written in her diary after completing *Night and Day:* "I suppose I lay myself open to the charge of niggling with emotions that don't really matter."[34] In *A Passage to India,* Forster comments on the low intensity of the average consciousness; he may well have made the same point to Virginia Woolf in person.[35]

But in spite of her own second thoughts and the comments of her friends, *Jacob's Room* did represent significant achievement. In it Virginia Woolf had, by the selection and vivid imitation of sensory experience and fleeting minor actions, brought to the reader a keen sense of the beauty and the "agitation" of life. She had developed structural support for the plot which also serves thematically, although the patterns of imagery are not always clearly related to the action of search. She had worked out, although not made full use of, the dramatization of her characters' consciousness. And though she had not succeeded to her own critical satisfaction in creating an aesthetic whole with the emotional power to make its form unmistakably clear, she had made a final break from the conclusive plot of reconciliation that she attempted in *Night and Day*.

chapter Seven

A very finely considered balance:
Mrs. Dalloway

Mrs. Dalloway *was published in London at the Hogarth Press* in 1925. Virginia Woolf began it as a short story in August 1922, and it emerged at last, after long months of exploration, as a novel that she said, left her "plunged deep in the richest strata of my mind."[1] It has, like all her fiction, a plot of search, a structure of contrasts, and a perspective of amply developed dualism. It is the account of a June day in London, 1923; its middle-aged society heroine, Clarissa Dalloway, is called on by an old suitor, Peter Walsh; she plans and gives a fashionable party; a deranged young war veteran, Septimus Warren Smith, commits suicide rather than submit to the bullying of his doctors. Social worlds apart, never meeting in the flesh, these two protagonists each seek for and find a way to preserve their inner freedom in a world where order is both an admirable tradition and the grounds for intolerable coercion; they are the sane and the insane manifestation of the same passion for an inviolable private vision of life. In *Mrs. Dalloway,* Virginia Woolf realizes a persuasive form controlled by her complex perspective and attains as well her goals of humanity, depth, and emotional power. In short, for the first time she brings into a powerfully effective balance the conflicting forces that characterize the world of her fiction.

She attacks again all the problems of balance, thematic and technical, that she had faced in the past. She returns to the ambiguous view of order and disorder of *The Voyage Out.* She enriches this view and dramatizes it by fusing the natural and symbolic representation of experience simultaneously in the characters' consciousness and by making the background characters, who represent "life" in *Jacob's Room,* embodiments of freedom or stability as well. She makes good use of the plotting skills learned in *Night and Day,* acknowledging from the beginning of the novel's composition the need for expectation and outer action that she did not supply in *Jacob's Room.* For the most part she omits lengthy and precious authorial comment, although she retains the privilege of making asides that clarify action and provide irony. She infuses characters with mythic connotations as she did in *The Voyage Out* and *Jacob's Room,* yet she establishes their particularity when this quality is necessary for interest and motivation. Throughout the novel she skillfully develops the binding metaphor of a web of shared vitality that related the seemingly disparate details of *Jacob's Room.* Significantly for the novel's emotional power, she uses the painful personal experience of her mental illness without self-pity or over-distancing.

The flaws of *Mrs. Dalloway* result from two problems of balance not perfectly solved: the relation between form and idea breaks down upon occasion and makes room for didactic peroration, and the double view of Clarissa sometimes weakens the reader's sympathy for her. But since both these problems are delicate matters of equilibrium, and since her solution of them can be supported in the light of the novel's perspective, they generate moot critical questions.

No schematization can exhaust the experience or fully describe the form of a work of art, but any "system" of viewing *Mrs. Dalloway* is more than ordinarily unsatisfactory since, because of the novel's economy, each of its technical devices simultaneously accomplishes a number of ends. The overlapping of categories must continually be acknowledged, for an image that conveys an acute sensory experience may also stand for an aspect of the perspective, and it may at the same time forward the action by recalling a memory that also characterizes and illuminates the present moment. In one brief paragraph, Clarissa Dalloway, recalling the lake on the grounds of her girlhood home, sees a dreamlike vision of the relationship between her past and the present mundane moment that enlarges the meaning of both:

> "Do you remember the lake?" she said, in an abrupt voice, under the pressure of an emotion which caught her heart, made the muscles of her throat stiff, and contracted her lips in a spasm as she said "lake." For she was a child throwing bread to the ducks, between her parents, and at the same time a grown woman coming to her parents who stood by the lake, holding her life in her arms which, as she neared them, grew larger and larger in her arms, until it became a whole life, a complete life, which she put down by them and said, "This is what I have made of it! This!" And what had she made of it? What, indeed? sitting there sewing this morning with Peter [p. 48].

Virginia Woolf said in retrospect that she had written the novel "as the oyster starts or the snail to secrete a house for itself . . . without any conscious direction."[2] But after ten weeks of work she did call a halt and set for herself clearly prescribed rules of economy and control. Her method of composing was always, after an original plan, to "dream into" a narrative, but she believed that *Jacob's Room* had suffered from too much improvisation and too little conscious control of structure and effect. Writing it, she had at one point chided herself for a lack of direction: "I have not thought my plan out plainly enough—so to dwindle, niggle, hesitate—which means that one's lost."[3] On October 29, 1922, she wrote: "I want to think out *Mrs. Dalloway.* I want to foresee this book better than the others and get the utmost out of it. I expect I could have screwed *Jacob* up tighter, if I had foreseen; but I had to make my path as I went."[4] She did indeed anticipate a final effect and develop the principles by which to achieve it, but the techniques by which to use her newly acquired freedom in a pattern of stricter order than that of *Jacob's Room* without losing its lifelike qualities had to be worked out line by line. "Think what a labour the first pages of *Mrs. Dalloway* were," she wrote later. "Each word distilled by a relentless clutch on my brain."[5]

Her preface to the Modern Library edition is subtly defensive, seemingly designed to refute such hostile critics as Wyndham Lewis who attributed the novel's form to Joyce's influence. *Mrs. Dalloway,* she insists firmly, was not the deliberate offspring of a method. "The little notebook in which an attempt was made to forecast a plan was soon abandoned, and the book grew day by day, week by week, without any plan at all, except that which was dictated each morning in the writing."[6] In the face of her diary entry of June 19 (*AWD,* p. 57), which marvels that the design is "so queer and so masterful," and that she must "wrench" her substance to fit it, this seems disingenuous. But the first forecasted plan contained subject matter and chapter divisions she did not use. The "design" was not a similar outline but a set of abstract principles by which, day by day and week by week, she governed the substance and order. A method had to be evolved along the way to fit the concept; the two statements are not really contradictory.

In the course of the writing, Clarissa split into Clarissa and Septimus; the resulting double plot subdivided into past and present sections. As a result, action and characterization were complicated by the necessity of moving between and simultaneously advancing four lines of development, all embedded in the vital passing moment of London life and by extension the life of the Empire. Because of this background, social criticism is implicit in the conflict between the inner and the outer obligations of Clarissa and Septimus. Half complaining of the burden of such widening complexity, Virginia Woolf wrote: "In this book I have almost too many ideas. I want to give life and death, sanity and insanity; I want to criticise the social system, and to show it at work, at its most intense."[7]

To bring together her diary notes on the progress of the novel, the holograph working notes, the short story version of the first section of the novel, and the long false start in the British Museum manuscript (which is cast as the experience of Peter Walsh) is to understand her continuing struggle to fuse the consciously imposed formal principles and the fruitful subconscious powers of invention. Often the consciously posed technical problem was solved by a sudden insight, as was her Proustlike "tunnelling process" of recalling memories that relate characters. She described this inspiration as the sudden release of imaginative powers.

She began the story "Mrs. Dalloway in Bond Street" as a necessary protection against her fear of being "clowned in public" by bad reviews of *Jacob's Room.* Such self-defense by diversion to new tasks was her common strategy; the period after completing a novel was ordinarily one of dangerous depression and discouragement. She wrote on August 16, 1922, that she was writing too quickly, that she must "press together" the story. On August 28 she noted her determination to finish it in a month, at the same time toying with the idea of extending it into a novel.

On October 4, shortly after reading *Ulysses,* she finished it, and it was published in the July 1923 issue of *Dial.* One uncharacteristic digression of the story, Mrs. Dalloway's ladylike musing on the physiology of the ageing matron, may indeed have been an experiment in the biological frankness of Molly Bloom, but it was later omitted from the novel. Her public defense for such self-censorship of the grosser aspects of the flesh was that men would be shocked by a woman's frank discussion of her body; as a result, the woman writer's creative imagination was blocked.[8] But her strong distaste for Joyce's cheerful and specific vulgarity was instinctive, a recoil deeply connected with her nature.

Only two days after finishing the story she decided to go on with it as a novel and entered a plan for its first two chapters in her notebook. There is no hint in the outline that follows of a narrative line; the concern is for structural relationship and subject matter:

> Thoughts upon beginning a book to be called, perhaps, At Home; or At the Party.

> This is to be a short book consisting of six or seven chapters, each complete separately. In them must be some fusion. And all must converge upon the party at the end. My idea is to have some characters, like Mrs. Dalloway, much in relief; then to have some interludes of thought or reflection, or moments of digression (which must be related, logically, to the next) all compact, yet not jerked.

> The chapters might be
> 1. Mrs. Dalloway in Bond Street
> 2. The Prime Minister
> 3. Ancestors

4. A dialogue
5. The old ladies
6. County house?
7. Cut flowers
8. The party

One, roughly to be done in a month; but this plan is to consist of some very short intervals, not whole chapters.

There should be fun.

On the reverse side of this notebook page is the plan for the second "interval," in which she develops by details the characteristic double vision of the scene as interplay between order and disorder.

P.M.

To give 2 points of view at once; authority and irresponsibility.
Authority prancing through the streets sending uneasiness to
    Gerard Street.
(diversion upon the respectable worldliness—from point of view of
    Scallywag who is looking at books.)
P.M. drives on.
Digression on china, French shops, Restaurants.
    Freedom-irresponsibility
       Contrast between thought and action
The guards changing
P.M. reaches Westminster
        (he has a card for the party)
The crowd assembled.

Mrs. D. a particular character.
P.M. generalized. Who is to represent the scally wags?
A man or a woman?
A man of the thoughtful class. Ugly. Not deformed.
Precious near it.[9]

Except for the mysterious last phrases, these notes as clues to the novel as we know it seem clear. The context of the action is the contrast between the Prime Minister and the scallywag: Clarissa is aligned with the Prime Minister's party. The scene is to be set against the elegant, worldly life of London.

Virginia Woolf did indeed write this section as a second chapter; its strongest effect was that of social criticism. It is an eighteen-page typescript in the Berg Collection, and it differs substantially from the final version. The Berg manuscript centers around a scallywag who appears only as a passing figure in the novel. Charles G. Hoffmann describes the abandonment of the explicit dramatization of class conflict as a major thematic shift that grew out of the introduction of Septimus Smith and the resulting widening of the novel's action.[10] The social comment does remain as a major element, although it is absorbed into the larger conflict between the individual and the social system played out in the lives of Clarissa and Septimus.

There is no question that the introduction of Septimus, who appears in the original "Prime Minister" version as a bizarre and mysterious figure, greatly enlarged the thematic range and increased the technical problems. The author's preface mentions the most critical shift in the plot plan: "In the first version Septimus, who later is intended to be her double, had no existence, . . . Mrs. Dalloway was originally to kill herself or perhaps merely to die at the end of the party."[11] On October 14, Virginia Woolf recorded her decision to use a double plot; most critics assume that because she was reading Joyce at this time, that Bloom and Stephen Daedalus offered her the pattern for Clarissa-Septimus, but she was also reading Dostoevsky and his doppelgangers seem a closer parallel. More pertinent to her inspiration perhaps is a letter that she wrote when she was twenty-one. The pattern of doubleness and failed consummation is in full harmony with her temperament and with the plot of *Mrs. Dalloway:*

> I'm going to write a great play which shall be all talk too. . . . that is a plan of mine and Jack's—we are going to write it together—it could be done, I'm sure—I'm going to have a man and woman—show them growing up—never meeting—not knowing each other—but all the time you'll feel them come nearer and nearer—this will be the real exciting part (as you see) but when they almost meet—only a door between—you see how they just miss & go off at a tangent & never come anywhere near again.[12]

In *Mrs. Dalloway,* Clarissa and Septimus, although without visible connections, do "come nearer and nearer." Clarissa is told of Septimus' suicide at her party; his doctor is her guest. And when she feels "somehow like him—the young man who killed himself," their kinship is illuminated; the fullness of our recognition has been prepared from the first pages (p. 204). On June 18, 1923, Virginia Woolf had made this note: "Every scene would build up the idea of C's character. That will give unity as well as add to the final effect."[13] The final effect is the party at which Clarissa, through her relationship to Septimus at the height of her own vitality, absorbs the experience of his death into the fullness of her understanding of life. The book's title as the summation of the book's experience becomes clear.

Such successfully created excitement results from Virginia Woolf's realization of the principles of her final working notes of October 16, 1922 (already quoted in part in Chapter 5). In them she succinctly acknowledges her determination to create the sympathy, expectancy, and inevitability of action traditional to the novel; she describes the comparison, balance, contrast, and harmony of the perspective and structure that she hopes to achieve; she states her decision to make the foreground of the action the dramatized consciousness of her characters. The only significant technical innovation of *Mrs. Dalloway* that she omits from this list is the constant movement between past and present. The memories of the characters, she wrote in her diary, were invented to create greater sympathy for Clarissa, whose shallowness and coldness seemed to detract from the emotional power of the story. These notes are the key to the masterful design:

A possible revision of this book

Suppose it to be connected in this way.
Sanity and insanity.
Mrs. D. is seeing the truth. Septimus seeing the insane truth.
The book is to have the intensity of a play; only in narrative.
Some revisions therefore needed.
At any rate, very careful composition.
The contrast must be arranged.

> Therefore, how much detail and digression?
> The pace to be given by a gradual increase of S.'s insanity on
>   one side, by the approach of the party on the other.
> The design is extremely complicated.
> The balance must be very finely considered.
> All to take place in one day?
> There must be excitement to draw one on.
> Also human
> The question is whether the inside of the mind in both Mrs. D.
>   and SS can be made luminous—that is to say the stuff
>   of the book—Lights on it coming from external sources.[14]

These "necessary" revisions begin with the first paragraph of the story.
In contrast to the novel's lively dramatization of Clarissa's thoughts, the
short story opens with authorial description:

> Mrs. Dalloway said she would buy the gloves herself.
> Big Ben was striking as she stepped out into the street. It was
> eleven o'clock and the unused hour was fresh as is issued to chil-
> dren on a beach. But there was something solemn in the deliberate
> swing of the repeated strokes; something stirring in the murmur of
> wheels and the shuffle of footsteps. No doubt they were not all
> bound on errands of happiness. There is much more to be said
> about us than that we walk the streets of Westminister. Big Ben is
> nothing but steel rods consumed by rust were it not for the care of
> H. M.'s Office of Works. Only for Mrs. Dalloway the moment was
> complete; for Mrs. Dalloway June was fresh.[15]

This commentary is not characteristic of the body of the story which is
chiefly successful interior monologue—Clarissa's reverie, intermittently
darkened by thoughts of death, as she meets Hugh Whitbread, buys
gloves, and thinks of England's past and her own. The narrator breaks
in chiefly to comment on Clarissa's life: "Pride held her erect, inherit-
ing, and handing on, acquainted with discipline and suffering" (p. 20).
Clarissa's own thoughts of that supporting past led her to thoughts of
death:

> For all the great things one must go to the past, she thought. From
> all the contagion of the world's slow stain. . . . Fear no more the

heat o' the sun. . . . And now can never mourn, she repeated, her eyes straying over the window; for it ran in her head; the test of great poetry; the moderns had never written anything one wanted to read about death, she thought, and turned [p. 23].

The story ends with a trick, like "The Mark on the Wall." There is a violent explosion in the street outside and Clarissa remembers the name of the woman at the opposite end of the glove counter. "But Clarissa, sitting very upright, smiled at the other lady. 'Miss Anstruther!' she exclaimed" (p. 27).

"Mrs. Dalloway on Bond Street" is a slice of life; in contrast, the parallel pages in the novel (pp. 5-16) are the background and beginning of a complex action in which almost every minor detail is related to details which follow. The writer must have constantly said to herself: "Suppose it to be connected in this way," for in the novel the choice of image is more critical; it must be capable of generating a chain reaction. In the short story a neighbor sees Clarissa pass: "A charming woman, poised, eager, strangely white-haired for her pink cheeks, so Scope Purvis, C.B., saw her as he hurried to his office" (p. 20). The similar passage in the novel is more imaginative: "A charming woman, Scope Purvis thought her (knowing her as one does know people who live next door to one in Westminster); a touch of the bird about her, of the jay, blue-green, light vivacious, though she was over fifty, and grown very white since her illness" (p. 6). The image makes possible our just appraisal of her less flattering birdlike self-image coming a few pages later. " 'She had a narrow pea-stick figure,' she thought, 'a ridiculous little face, beaked like a bird' " (p. 13). This likeness also binds her to the hawklike Septimus.

A more complicated sequence that connects both plots results from a seemingly trivial change between story and novel; Clarissa buys flowers rather than gloves. The flowers, which in the first paragraph of *Mrs. Dalloway* link her to "divine vitality," also prepare the scene in the florist's in which we gain a deeper sense of her identity with the living world. Later her response to flowers and plants connects her to Septimus Smith; next, Septimus' increasingly morbid identification with flowers charts the gradual growth of his insanity. First, Clarissa enters the shop to make her selection for the party:

There were flowers; delphiniums, sweet peas, bunches of lilac; and
carnations, masses of carnations. There were roses; there were
irises. Ah yes—so she breathed in the earthy garden sweet smell as
she stood talking to Miss Pym . . . turning her head from side to
side among the irises and roses and nodding tufts of lilac with her
eyes half closed, snuffing in, after the street uproar, the delicious
scent, the exquisite coolness . . . as if this beauty, this scent, this
colour, and Miss Pym liking her, trusting her, were a wave which
she let flow over her. . . [pp. 15-16].

Clarissa's sensory delight in merging with the flowers, although extraordinarily keen, is yet quite normal. She is "seeing the truth"—her
relationship with "life itself."

As parallel and contrast we first see Septimus Smith in the park. He
feels a similar but pathological response to the foliage about him; he is
convinced that his link with it is literal and physical. Septimus sees "the
insane truth." "But they beckoned; leaves were alive; trees were alive.
And the leaves being connected by millions of fibres with his own
body, there on the seat, fanned it up and down; when the branches
stretched he, too, made that statement" (p. 26). This unity becomes
more painful and threatening as his madness deepens: "The earth
thrilled beneath him. Red flowers grew through his flesh; their stiff
leaves rustled by his head" (p. 76). Again and again Clarissa and Septimus are related through such parallelisms of response, abnormally
heightened in Septimus.

Such multiple connections, however, the "very careful composition," the "arranged contrast," "the extremely complicated design,"
and "the finely considered balance" are all controlled not only by the
rationale of an aesthetic and associative pattern, but by the divided
perspective. Values in the novel are more complex than those of "Mrs.
Dalloway on Bond Street." In the story, Clarissa's thoughts of death are
a minor antiphonal strain alternating with the color and movement of
the bright June day, but in the novel death is simultaneously the enemy
of life and life's indivisible omnipresent alter ego; Clarissa sees herself,
dead or alive, as magically at one with the "ebb and flow of things." In
a definition even more dualistic than her view of death, Virginia Woolf
discriminates in the novel between the positive and negative aspects of a
value which is in the story a pure good—the power of tradition. In *Mrs.*

Dalloway tradition's potentiality for tyranny and dehumanization is explored as well as its power to preserve, inspire, unite, and "hand on." Clarissa resists the arrogance of institutions that invade the "privacy of the soul." She thinks: "For in marriage a little licence, a little independence there must be between people living together day in day out in the same house" (p. 10). And she resents the passion to convert that has changed her daughter's tutor, "burning, bitter" Doris Kilman, into a fanatic churchwoman. In Clarissa's vision, the climactic scene of the novel, she declares that life cannot be coerced: "Here was one room; there another. Did religion solve that, or love?"(P. 141.)

By such splitting up of values and emotions, as she calls it, Virginia Woolf arrives at the technical and thematic equipoise she sought. On the one hand, the variety of ideas, images, characters, and actions produced by the divisions creates the desired lifelike diversity and complexity. "Suppose one can keep the quality of a sketch in a finished and composed work?" she asked herself in the last stages of writing *Mrs. Dalloway*. [16] On the other hand, the interwoven oppositions of all this multiplicity make a finished and composed work possible, for they create both an aesthetic and a logical pattern of relationships.

The novel's doubled and opposed values form the social corollary of her aesthetic theory of balance. By implication the ideal life is a reconciliation of the positive aspects of both order and disorder.

The world of authority and order at its best evidences the qualities of form, tradition, duty, stoicism, community, and a sense of the past. When properly balanced by the freedom of the individual within its system, its order is fruitful, but it must not be allowed to destroy vitality, intuition, resilience, sensitivity, imagination, and gaiety. When either the Prime Minister or the Scallywag moves away toward an extreme position, there is chaos or tyranny. A mechanical and rigid social system permits coercion and encourages complacency, snobbery, and possessiveness; it is ultimately sterile. Irresponsible escapism, for all its charm, fails to reach its potential creativity and may end in disintegration. The negative character of either authority or freedom at its nadir is identical in human terms—a lack of sympathy.

In *Mrs. Dalloway*, the ideal balance is not achieved. Clarissa's reconciling act, the party giving, is marred by triviality and egotism; the temporary order established by the party contains traces of ambitious coldness. Septimus Smith's rejection of tyranny by self-destruction is heroic excess; ultimate rebellion against the coercion of the social order destroys him. *Mrs. Dalloway* is a world, not a system; what distinguishes it is the imaginative power and the lifelike variety by which conventional dualities are embodied, related, and opposed and by which life, flawed and divided, is affirmed.

The two main plots are complementary. The quest of Clarissa's day is composed of compromises between the world of authority and of her own love of freedom as she seeks to evaluate her own existence. She accuses herself of lack of feeling. Septimus searches for truth in a nightmare life, distorted by his conviction that the world had condemned him to death because he could not feel.

Clarissa admits to scheming and to social ambition, but like the Lady of the Magic Garden in Virginia Woolf's early fairy story, she had "that extraordinary gift, that woman's gift, of making a world of her own wherever she happened to be" (p. 85). Withdrawing from her party, Clarissa experiences her vision alone; she senses her identity with Septimus, who has rebelled against the outer life; she honors the sublimity of his death; she reflects on the eternal loneliness of human life. At the party meanwhile, her friends discuss her faults, but when she rejoins them, she is filled with power, a hostess so magical, so life-loving, that she brings terror and ecstasy to the heart of Peter Walsh: "It is Clarissa, he said. For there she was" (p. 213).

The plot of Clarissa's past, a love story that emerges in fragments through her memories and those of Peter, is more outwardly and conventionally dramatic than the story of her day. We learn its climax before we are given its details. Clarissa remembers: "that scene in the little garden by the fountain, she had to break with him or they would have been destroyed, both of them ruined, she was convinced; though she had borne about in her for years like an arrow sticking in her heart, the grief, the anguish" (p. 10). Peter's pain, too, is felt through his account, in which we come to know not only Clarissa's coldness but Peter's feckless romantic susceptibility and the possessiveness to which she will not submit. Weak and attractive, he stands for the romantic position and implicitly confirms the wisdom of Clarissa's decision, although her life errs on the side of decorous frigidity.

Both plots, past and present, bring Clarissa to a climactic act of balancing inner and outer obligations. Her solution is imperfect; she sometimes lacks spontaneous warmth. Her character is specified by the faults, but at the same time she is enlarged and deified as she moves among her guests: "Lolloping on the waves and braiding her tresses she seemed, having that gift still; to be; to exist; to sum it all up in a moment as she passed" (p. 191). One of the critical questions in evaluating this novel is: Can Clarissa, a little snobbish, more than a little cool, wear this crown with conviction? (Virginia Woolf's own ambivalence toward the world of fashion—half entranced, half mocking—complicated the characterization.)[17]

The figure of Septimus Smith, too, is mythic and magnified. Paranoid and prophetic, he is "a scapegoat, the eternal sufferer"; in his tormented visions he is one "lately taken from life to death, the Lord who had come to renew society" (p. 29). He is also a young clerk, late a British soldier in Italy, who has lost his best friend, Evans, near the close of the war and shortly after married a little Italian milliner, Lucrezia. The climax in the reprise of his past is the onset of his illness—the pathological loss of feeling by a man naturally sensitive and empathetic. But soon came "the thunderclaps of fear . . . he could not feel" (p. 98). His illness is the hellish distortion of emotions and alienation and guilt. The grossly hearty Dr. Holmes accuses him of cowardice and recommends porridge and cricket for mental health. Sir William Bradshaw, the Harley Street specialist, urges upon him "a sense of proportion" and arranges to send him to a nursing home. So, although Septimus thinks "Life was good," he throws himself "vigorously, violently" out of his window to escape "that brute, Humanity." "The fallen, he said, they tear to pieces" (p. 155).

The plots of Clarissa and Septimus unfold discontinuously and gradually; the past takes shape in nonchronological order through memories. The searching action is constant; Peter Walsh asks eternal questions: "What is it? Where am I? And, why, after all, does one do it?" (P. 58.) And the reader does not have to await the culmination of the suicide or the party to experience and understand the conflict of values through which the quest for revelation must be made. Directly and emotionally, from the first page on, he is exposed, even bombarded by, the sensory experience of the main characters that teems with images and persons who manifest desirable and undesirable forms of order and disorder. Beginning the novel, Virginia Woolf had written: "I feel I can use up everything I ever thought."[18] All her richness and fertility of imagination were needed to prevent the complicated pattern she envisioned from destroying the novel's sense of life. In the last stages of writing she spoke of "spurts of thought, coming as I walk, as I sit; things churning up in my mind and so making a perpetual pageant."[19] The multiplicity of the pageant's details and the complexity of their interrelationship were brought into a balance that produced the freedom and the control for which she had so persistently striven.

The perpetual pageant is more emotionally powerful in *Mrs. Dalloway* than in *Jacob's Room* not only because it is shown on "the inside of the mind," but because what she called the "splitting" of values produced ethical contrasts more dynamic than the alternation of immobility and flux in the earlier novel. Sergei Eisenstein's discussion of montage is again helpful here. Effective montage, he says, works "like a series of explosions" in an internal combustion engine, driving the film forward. Each shot must develop an emotional intensity that shatters the frame and leads to the next shot.[20] In *Mrs. Dalloway* the images are indeed explosive rather than static, as they are in *Jacob's Room,* because they represent the ethical antitheses in the lives of the protagonists who must live within the social system and yet maintain the privacy of their souls. The "pageant" dramatizes the search for balance.

She achieves the necessary variety by ranging images and characters, not only by values, both pure and mixed, but along a spectrum of gradually increasing particularity. No highly conscious scheme is posited as a creative method; her imagination worked fruitfully with her belief. The scale begins with the natural imagery and culminates in Clarissa and Septimus, who are both complex specified characters and protean identities that participate in all life. Clarissa says to herself, riding the bus up Shaftsbury Avenue: "she felt herself everywhere; not 'here, here, here'; and she tapped the back of the seat; but everywhere" (p. 168). All details are joined by a web of vitality. Lady Bruton falling asleep feels: "as if one's friends were attached to one's body, after lunching with them, by a thin thread" (p. 124).

Nine years earlier Virginia Woolf had spoken in a book review of the desirability of realizing in fiction "a quickened perception of the relations existing between men and plants, or houses and their inhabitants, or any one of those innumerable alliances which somehow or other we spin between ourselves and other objects in our passage."[21] In *Mrs. Dalloway* such alliances are created by the sense of beauty, continuity, and mutability. Peter Walsh, walking to Clarissa's party, experiences such a quickened perception:

> The windows lit up, a piano, a gramophone sounding; a sense of pleasure-making hidden, but now and again emerging, when, through the uncurtained window, the window left open, one saw parties sitting over tables, young people slowly circling, conversations between men and women, maids idly looking out (a strange comment theirs when work was done), stockings drying on top ledges, a parrot, a few plants. Absorbing, mysterious, of infinite richness, this life [pp. 179-180].

The novel is a tissue of such glimpses interwoven with the images of memory. Through the shifting scene the action is placed in the context of all time and all life, ruled over by the eternal mythical female figures of the street singer and the gray nurse of death knitting in the park.

The life cast in general forms is rich and various; in its individual manifestations it is also irresponsible and seeks escape. The airplane, to which all on Bond Street raise their eyes, is "a symbol . . . of man's soul; of his determination, thought Mr. Bentley, sweeping round the cedar tree, to get outside his body, beyond his house, by means of thought" (p. 32). And this willful irresponsibility may be as disruptive as the passion of Peter Walsh, who at fifty-three is arranging a divorce for the young wife of a fellow officer so that he may marry her although he knows in the growing selfishness of age he will neglect her.

There are various levels or increasing degrees of particularization in the delineation of the supernumeraries, vignettes, stereotypes, and complex characters who are on the side of the free, the life-loving, and the scallywags. There are such nameless figures as "the veriest frumps, the most dejected of miseries sitting on doorsteps (drink their downfall) who can't be dealt with . . . by Acts of Parliament for that very reason: they love life" (p. 6); such montage shots as that of Moll Pratt, prepared to throw a bunch of roses, the price of a pot of beer, into the street to honor royalty; and the more clearly detailed Mrs. Dempster, on a park bench, pulling her knobbed feet beneath her and musing like Clarissa: "But whether I'd have chosen like that if I'd known," and recommending the art of balance: "better to be a little stout, a little slack, a little moderate in one's expectations" (p. 31).

Such vital characters who never reappear are tied to the major characters by the similarity of their response to life. Young Maisie Johnson, up to London from the country for the first time, walks through the park timidly. She is as unformed as Clarissa's daughter Elizabeth, unawakened and lovely, who plays a more important role in defining the private life of the young who are not yet part of the social machine. On a more particularized level of the scallywags are Sally Seton, the rash friend of Clarissa's girlhood, and Peter Walsh, who have the double function of acting out the attractiveness and volatility of the free spirit and of illuminating Clarissa's compromise with the world of the Prime Minister.

The permutations and levels of order in the novel are more complex than those of disorder, for in this aspect of human life Virginia Woolf reveals the strength and weakness of institutions and tradition. On the positive side, the Prime Minister's car magically unites the bystanders in an emotion of loyalty to "the enduring symbol of the state"; the thought of Empire moves all hearts; the vision of St. Paul's gives balm and welcome, an image of "tombs with banners waving over them" (p. 32); young men march by, "on their faces an expression like the letters of a legend written round the base of a statue praising duty, gratitude, fidelity, love of England" (p. 57). Clarissa's home is a shrine of ritual and decorum over which she rules. But the characters who stand for aspects of order become more mixed and less attractive as they become more particularized. The minor figures, Lady Bexborough, "slow and stately, rather large, interested in politics like a man," and Sir John Buckhurst, the old Judge, are wholly admirable (p. 13). But Lady Bruton, more fully developed, is complacent, domineering, limited; Hugh Whitbread, for all his manners and breeding, is pompous, arrogant, and stupid. Only Richard Dalloway, not quite first-rate but dutiful, is an appealing figure of order. The three representatives of Conversion, or persuasion by force, the form of ordering that "feasts on the will of others," are Doris Kilman, Dr. Holmes, and Sir William Bradshaw. Miss Kilman, wretched and unlovable, is furnished with a past that explains her pitiable lack of charm. But the two doctors are monsters of egotistical aggression for whom no excuse can be made. In their characterization alone, of all the more fully developed figures, the narrator does not follow Clarissa's rule about the complexity of people; "She would not say of anyone in the world that they were this or that"

(p. 10). Even such an unimportant character as Hugh Whitbread is given from diverse angles of judgment, as both dutifully conscientious and tiresomely petty.

All this large cast, particularized or general, as emblems of authority or irresponsibility, performs in an action of alternation that was analyzed by David Daiches in *The Novel and the Modern World* (1960). His diagram shows the regular contrast of an interlude in which time stands still and a variety of characters are shown in simultaneous action followed invariably by a longer interlude in which the chief focus is the consciousness of a major character which moves back and forth in time. This is the "contrast between thought and action" which Virginia Woolf's original plan had predicted—like that of *Jacob's Room,* yet far less episodic in effect. Connecting this structure of contrasting narrative techniques is the sound of two London bells: Big Ben, "shredding, slicing, subdividing" time relentlessly, and St. Margaret's, which unites minds mysteriously, like Clarissa herself, Peter thinks, gliding "into the recesses of the heart" (p. 56). The bells often make possible a shift in point of view; they always contrast clock time and mind time. In short, every possible device of contrast and relationship by which the various experience of many minds can be fused and dovetailed is used.

But besides making possible the movement of the action in time and space, the structure works in a conventional way to control sympathy and to develop emotional climax. Since the form and power of the novel depends on its emotion, the question of Virginia Woolf's ability to balance between sentimentality and coldness in delineating Clarissa and Septimus is critical.

Theoretically, Septimus Smith would seem to pose the greatest difficulty. Virginia Woolf herself was wary of trying to use her own mental illness as raw material. "Of course the mad part tries me so much, makes my mind squirt so badly that I can hardly face spending the next weeks at it."[22] Rewriting at the last she confesses dread at returning to it. But her method of rendering the distortions of Septimus' mind without pitying his state directly maintains him on a heroic level and avoids the danger of bathos. His mental sufferings are rendered in striking imagery: "Why could he see through bodies, see into the future when dogs will become men? It was the heat wave presumably, operating upon a brain made sensitive by eons of evolution. Scientifically speaking, the flesh was melted off the world. His body was macerated until only the nerve fibers were left. It was spread like a veil upon a rock" (p. 76). The pity is diverted to his little Italian wife, exiled, frightened, bewildered alike by his withdrawal and wildness and by the conflicting reports of the doctors. The notebook plan for her characterization reads: "Septimus must be seen by someone. His wife? She is to be bounded in S. Simple, instinctive, childless. She is to be a real character. He is only real as far as she sees him. Otherwise to exist in his view of things; which is always to be contrasting with Mrs. Dalloway's."[23] But there is much in Septimus' past which Rezia does not know and which he, in his hectic state, cannot rationally remember; therefore, the narrator must assume more expository duties in the Septimus plot than in the Clarissa plot. The villainous doctors, whose flaws Rezia can sense but not analyze, must be treated to some degree by the narrator. However, it is in performing this office that she loses control, intruding redundant direct attack that is already effectively implicit in the action. The long digression in which Sir William Bradshaw becomes the symbol of intolerable tyranny escalates into a harangue. The furious condemnation is in perfect harmony with the values of the novel, but it turns Sir William Bradshaw into a caricature, denying the novel's insistence on human complexity. It is the preaching Virginia Woolf complained of in D. H. Lawrence.

There are clear reasons for her antipathy to the medical profession. Her distrust of their competence appears in an early letter to Violet Dickinson, even before Thoby's death and her own most serious illness: "I shall never believe anything any doctor says—I learnt their utter helplessness when Father was ill. They can guess at what's the matter, but they can't get it right."[24] There are two doctors in the novel whose diagnoses diametrically disagree; both do irreparable harm to the patient.

Virginia Woolf had been shipped off to nursing homes by a family physician whom Leonard Woolf describes as a man of the world much like Sir William Bradshaw. In the midst of the outburst in the novel the narrator writes scornfully: "Worshipping proportion, Sir William not only prospered himself but made England prosper, secluded her lunatics, forbade childbirth, penalized despair, made it impossible for the unfit to propagate their views until they, too, shared his sense of proportion" (pp. 110-111). Virginia Woolf had been forbidden childbirth, and Leonard Woolf explains his full agreement with the wisdom of this verdict; but two letters to Violet Dickinson during the first year of the marriage show that Mrs. Woolf, no matter how soberly she acquiesced to the interdiction, was at this time either still hopeful of bearing a child or unwilling to acknowledge the decision as final. Quentin Bell records that her childlessness was always a source of misery and envy. Doctors were inextricably associated with her deepest sufferings.

But the satiric tirade against the doctors in *Mrs. Dalloway*, so keenly felt, is not a serious aesthetic flaw. It relieves the reader's own indignation against the insensitive treatment of Septimus Smith, and her original plan had been to have "some digression." The central problem of the novel's power is not in the development of Septimus' mortal plight, but in the concept of Clarissa's character. Is the discrepancy between her mundane and her mythic selves too great? The social Clarissa, Peter believes, has become over the years sentimental and cold. Her own musings show her to be sexually frigid, her spontaneous lesbian impulses repressed. Yet she is also a Goddess of Life, gathering and unifying its manifestations in every form. No extravagant claims are made for her ultimate power; the party accomplishes little but a temporary illumination, although Clarissa experiences a moment of vision. Her response to the world, joyful and intense, is made movingly real. She does not, however, command unqualified sympathy from the reader. But, it is important to see that her heartlessness is in keeping with the central theme of "the death of the soul" in the world that she chooses; her coldness is tied to the fatal coldness of Septimus, also brought about by the failure of that world in warring.

Virginia Woolf herself saw this lack of sympathetic appeal in Clarissa and at one stage almost abandoned the novel on this account. Reconsidering the matter after its completion, she blamed her difficulty on her own dislike of her model for the character, Kitty Maxse: "I found Clarissa in some way tinselly. . . . I think some distaste for her persisted. Yet, again, that was true to my feeling for Kitty and one must dislike people in art without its mattering, unless indeed it is true that certain characters detract from the importance of what happens to them."[25]

The use of a live prototype for characterization was not a departure for her. Virginia Woolf's novels were all, to some degree, *romans à clef.*

This fact may have contributed to her acute distress before the first intended publication of *The Voyage Out,* which contained the Ambroses and Rachel—very like her parents and herself, an unflattering likeness to Lytton Strachey, and even the revenge upon reality of her account of what seems to have been an actual episode, her "illicit kiss" from a married man. Lytton Strachey appears again as Neville in *The Waves;* Katherine Hilberry of *Night and Day* resembles herself, as she intended; Mrs. Hilberry is a recognizable Lady Anne Ritchie, charming and addled.

Kitty Maxse did indeed inspire both Clarissa Dalloways. However, Virginia Woolf was never tied to her model; the characters in both novels are refashioned and molded to function in a particular way in a particular fictional world. Mrs. Maxse was, as Jacqueline Latham reports in *Notes and Queries,* "a very attractive and dominating older woman" whom Virginia had known from her youth.[26] She had a part in the disastrous and quickly abandoned attempt to launch Vanessa and Virginia in society after their father's death. Both young ladies were beautiful and formidable, gauche and fiercely shy. Neither felt at home in the beau monde. Although Vanessa and Kitty remained friends, Virginia never liked her, but entertained a kind of jealous admiration for her charm. Helen Ambrose in *The Voyage Out* speaks a little bitterly of Clarissa, saying that all men really prefer women to be fashionable. And the Clarissa of the first novel is fashionable indeed—pretty, inconsistent, ardent, uninformed, and given to such clichés of enthusiasm as "I adore Bach." But there is in her no trace of domination; her role is to demonstrate to Rachel the role of the wife as worshipper, a woman limited to a state of such relaxing ignorance that her husband may enjoy nightly respite from the strain of his career. Clarissa Dalloway as a character has been perfectly developed to play her part in Rachel's exploration of values rather than as a picture of the "dominating" Kitty Maxse, who may in part have inspired her creation.

But Mrs. Maxse's life certainly had something to do with that aspect of the second Mrs. Dalloway which prompts from the author what A. D. Moody calls "a steady judgment of her deep inadequacy, a grave insistence upon the death of her spirit in glittering triviality."[27] She also owes something to the model of Lady Ottoline Morrell, however, as the author's diary notes; Lady Ott's propensity for self-serving and showy acts of generosity was responsible for Clarissa's trait of doing things to make people like her. Lytton Strachey, who did not like the book, believed it suffered from a "discordancy." Virginia Woolf notes his comment in her diary: "This is caused, he thinks, by some discrepancy in Clarissa herself; he thinks she is disagreeable and limited, but that I alternately laugh at her and cover her, very remarkably, with myself."[28] He could not have avoided noticing both Clarissa's characteristically Woolfian sensitivity to the experience and her equally characteristic frigidity that complicates the creation of sympathy for her as a feminine life-lover.

Yet, in the end, we must observe that the gravest charges against Clarissa are those that, in the self-knowledge of her fiftieth year, she makes against herself. This honesty acts in her favor; far from sentimental, as Peter pettishly calls her, she readily admits that her response to the present rose is more real than her interest in the far-off benighted Albanian. Clarissa's party nourishes the human need for beauty and for reassurance, and in her moment of triumph she is both an artist and a seer.

As always, Virginia Woolf took the first blows of criticism while launched on a new project. And she herself was not satisfied with Clarissa's power to arouse feeling. Beginning *To the Lighthouse* with a "quick flourishing attack," she set herself the task of achieving deeper emotion, critical to form and balance: "I want to learn greater quiet and force. But if I set myself that task, don't I run the risk of falling into the flatness of *N. & D.?* Have I got the power needed if quiet is not to become insipid?"[29]

chapter Eight

Economy and emotion: *To the Lighthouse*

Virginia Woolf described her typical mood upon finishing a novel as inhospitable to her creation; she was busy thinking of another work. But far from being feeling inhospitable to *To the Lighthouse* upon its completion, she pronounced it "easily the best" of her books, having decided as she brought it to a close that "it is subtler and more human than *Jacob's Room* and *Mrs. Dalloway*."[1] She had written it with the greatest ease of her experience. The fluency gave her the assurance that she was "on the right path."[2] At the time of its publication in 1927 she worried that she was not planning another novel: "I have no idea yet of any other to follow it: which may mean that I have made my method perfect and it will now stay like this and serve whatever use I wish to put it to."[3]

Critics and friends alike agreed that she had reached a high point. E. M. Forster wrote to her:

It's awfully sad, very beautiful, both in non-radiant color and shape, it stirs me much more to questions of whither and why than anything else you have written. The uneasiness of life seems to well up between all the words. The excitement of life on the other hand to be observed, stated. This I believe to be right; excitement would dry up all those little winds. I must read it again—am inclined to think it your best work.[4]

The growing reputation of the novel over the years supports her claim to a perfected technical balance and to the realization of deeper emotion. Its popularity has steadily increased as well. Giving evidence in his tribute to its importance, Leonard Woolf, always soberly practical, quoted sales figures: during the first three years following its publication, 11,763 copies of *To the Lighthouse* were sold in Britain and America; in the three years following 1965 the sales were 152,913 copies. In a comment even more indicative of the novel's power to move the common reader, he speaks of the great number of personal letters he was still receiving from its admirers in 1968.[5]

Critical visions and revisions continue to appear. Some, like David Daiches, have reversed earlier judgments and presently find *Mrs. Dalloway* more aesthetically satisfying than *To the Lighthouse*. Ruth Z. Temple, agreeing, attributes the latter's popularity to its appealing subject matter and judges its structural asymmetry and its shift of emphasis serious flaws, resulting from the writer's loss of control of the novel's original concept.[6] Explications and interpretations have radically changed since the first naive readings that saw Mrs. Ramsay as a martyr and Mr. Ramsay as a villain. Both these characters and their relationship have been shown, through careful studies such as those of Mitchell Leaska, to be more complex than early critics saw them to be.[7] And so, although any analysis of such a deeply read novel as *To the Lighthouse* must be in part a palimpsest of many sound and nonexclusive studies, one more examination of the novel as the culmination of Virginia Woolf's first phase may yet yield new insights. In short, *To the Lighthouse* is still mysterious and fruitful; it still provokes critical controversy; and another view of its techniques, its devices of economy and emotion, can offer insights into her work as a whole.

In this novel Virginia Woolf creates a scene, an action, characters, and ambiguously symbolic imagery perfectly suited to her own perspective. From beginning to end the authorial choices are in harmony both with her vision of life and with her definition of fictional form and effect. The novel's physical and psychic worlds compel belief; we can hear and feel the sea and enter the minds of the characters, never doubting the full reality of either. Inner and outer experiences complement and enrich each other. The world of an island, out of time, threatened by the encroachment of the tides, provides the natural poetic images; their connotations are suited to the symbolic action of a search for meaning, carried on by the rhythms of ecstasy and foreboding. The randomness of life is felt through the triviality of the surface events and through the instability of the resolution. But the expectation of the quest, the proposed voyage to the lighthouse, from the first page on, is a goal toward which the reader's eye is trained, further satisfying the author's definition of significant form.

The single plot is the gradual discovery of the complexity of the two main characters, Mr. and Mrs. Ramsay, a progressive balancing of the reader's initial emotional impressions of them, and the discovery of how their lives may shed light on the artist's quest for meaning. The reader's original simplistic response—that Mrs. Ramsay unequivocably deserves his sympathy and loyalty—is modified. The peace brought about by her outer actions is moving; she heals and comforts, feeds and shelters, knits up, revives, visits the sick. Yet the springs of vanity which in part nourish her generosity and the narrowness of her frame of reference are gradually revealed as her inner life is dramatized. Though she is a source of life and a familiar of death, her solutions are bounded by the character of her own social role. Mr. Ramsay's acts are abrasive; he shatters the composure of others by imposing rational order on their comforting fantasies or by invading their solitude to demand attention and pity; he is indifferent to the natural beauty of the world and to the feelings of those around him. Yet the dramatization of his inner life shows his intellectual integrity and his love of his family. He continues to irritate, but he wins respect. The novel implies that the ideal life would be a marriage of their best qualities, but no hope of this is extended. Only Lily Briscoe's painting of the final scene achieves such balance.

The relationship of Mr. and Mrs. Ramsay, their emotional effect on those around them, and Lily's growing understanding of both develop

the themes of human mystery, of egotism and dominance, of the creativity and limitations of sympathy, of the objectifying powers of reason and art, of the desirability of the androgynous life, and of the
omnipresent pressures of life and death that are central in all Virginia
Woolf's novels. There is brilliantly effective economy in the action, and
the transference of the order-disorder opposition from the complexities
of the social system to inner ambivalences and the conflicts of a marriage makes the tensions both more subtle and more human, as the
author herself observed. Mr. and Mrs. Ramsay reveal through both
thought and action the inherent weakness of pushing a single means of
conceiving experience to an egotistical extreme; neither intuition nor
reason alone can penetrate life. The two major figures elegantly encom-
pass the positive and negative aspects of both authority and individuality examined in the many characters of *Mrs. Dalloway*. What is more
important, they have great power to excite emotion.

For in *To the Lighthouse* Virginia Woolf uses with technical assurance those memories of her own childhood productive of deep feeling,
re-creating their physical and psychological reality with sensitivity,
courage, and control. She is working with highly volatile material, dangerous to her own stability, yet she does not distance herself from it
either by conventional, shallow sentimentality or by egotistical, divorced coolness. Her diary explicitly states that her parents were the
prototypes for Mr. and Mrs. Ramsay and that there was particular
emotional urgency behind their fictional resurrection. Writing of Leslie
Stephen in 1928, she said: "I used to think of him and mother
daily. . . . (I believe this to be true—that I was obsessed by them both,
unhealthily; and writing of them was a necessary act)."[8] The as yet
unpublished memoir, "A Sketch of the Past" (1939), describes her
parents' marriage as "equal" and "valiant," and limns the world of her
childhood as a crowded, merry, spinning whole. Yet to free herself
from the haunting questions of her parents' actual adult identities, she
explored the mysteries of their human weaknesses and exorcised them
as dominating ghosts. Their flaws were explored; the drama of their
marriage's conflict was deepened.

Their characters were changed and shaped to fill their function in
the novel's world, but they were particularized from vivid memories to
discover general human truths. It was as though Virginia Woolf was
saying what Lily Briscoe thought in another context: "If only she could

put them together, she felt, write them out in some sentence, then she could have gotten at the truth of things" (p. 219).

To write out her mother in one sentence was particularly difficult for the forty-three-year-old Virginia Woolf. Profoundly moved by Vanessa Bell's recognition of the portrait of Julia Stephen in Mrs. Ramsay, Virginia Woolf wrote her: "But what do you think I knew about mother? It can't have been much. What would Quentin have known of you if you had died when he was 13? I suppose one broods over some germ, but I specially refrained either from reading her letters or father's life. He was easier to do, But I was very much afraid of being sentimental."[9] And a few days later she wrote again:

> I'm in a terrible state of pleasure that you should think Mrs. Ramsay so like mother. At the same time, it's a psychological mystery why she should be; how a child could know about her, except that she has always haunted me, partly, I suppose, her beauty and then dying at that moment, I suppose she cut a great figure on one's mind when it was just awake and had not any experience of life—only then one would have suspected that one had made up a sham—an ideal.[10]

She admitted that Mrs. Ramsay was in part Vanessa; critics see the author herself in the associative patterns of Mrs. Ramsay's thinking, "merging, flowing, and creating." She was an imaginative synthesis of great complexity, not an effort toward perfect verisimilitude. The detailed portrait of Julia Stephen in "A Sketch of the Past," while never idealized, shows great admiration for her at last fatally expended strength. There is little hint of power-seeking in this account, although Julia's confidence and firmness are there.

Virginia Woolf had more abundant evidence for understanding her father, although creating a likeness of him in a character could not have been simple, either. She knew herself to be like him—in her hypersensitivity, her intellectual hunger, her propensity to withdraw, and her dependence on praise. All similarities made her both empathetic and critical. She had shared, with less intensity, her brother Adrian's and her sister Vanessa's angry rebellion against Leslie Stephen's mournful, domineering, self-pitying, self-dramatizing widower's rule in her adolescence. Obviously her feelings were deeply split, but her love for him was strong. She feared too tender a description.

In part the emotional power of her novel is her direct and courageous use of such disturbing material. To compare her delineation of her parents as characters in *To the Lighthouse* with their prototypes Mr. and Mrs. Ambrose in *The Voyage Out* reveals a gain in honesty and force. Mr. Ambrose, of course, was not central to the action. Moreover, she had deliberately muted, divided, and diffused her feelings about her parents in the earlier re-creation. Mr. Ramsay is a domestic tyrant, but Mr. Ambrose is only egocentric and irritable. The attacks on parental despotism are directed against the shadowy figure of Rachel's father. Helen Ambrose, regarding her brother-in-law coolly, is reported as thinking: "She suspected him of nameless atrocities with regard to his daughter; as indeed she had always suspected him of bullying his wife" (p. 24). In confidences to Rachel, Richard Dalloway complains of the injustices inflicted on him by his father, but the theme of domestic oppression is touched on only obliquely; it is so minor in this novel as to lack clear relevance to Rachel's life or character and adds no emotional power to the action.

Similarly, Virginia Woolf avoids in *The Voyage Out* any judgment of the mother figures. But judgment was a gnawing question. Despite her worshipful memories of Julia Stephen and her avowed longing for "maternal protectiveness" from other women, which she confessed to Violet Dickinson, she suspected the unconscious motives behind generosity in any person of power. In her mock biography of Violet, she asks these questions about her friend, a woman as intuitive and generous as Julia Stephen: "Did she reason or did she only instincticize? Where does care for others become care for oneself and at what point in her relationship with _____ [sic] did she cross the boundary of selfishness and become the most selfish of all living creatures?"[11] This is the query implicitly posed about Mrs. Ramsay throughout *To the Lighthouse*. It undercuts one's sense of what Lily called her "perfect goodness." In one typescript of *The Voyage Out*, in a passage later deleted, the same question is asked and abandoned as Rachel remembers her dead mother: "Such traits in her mother she feared and loved; and now she would never have to judge them—were they good or bad? because all such incidents when a person of such magnitude dies, are as sparks from one immense furnace, enduring, inexplicable as the sun."[12]

In a letter to her sister, however, written close to the publication of *To the Lighthouse*, Virginia Woolf showed that she had made some judgments on the potential warping ruthlessness of powerful maternity:

> I'm sure to return to your letter, that I should make a vile mother.
> For one thing (though this I try to hide from you) I slightly dis-
> trust or suspect the maternal passion. It is obviously immeasurable
> and unscrupulous. You would fry us all to cinders to give Angelica
> a day's pleasure without knowing it. You are a mere tool in the
> hands of passion. Other mothers are much worse and I've no doubt
> I should be worst of all. . . . appall me when they talk of their
> children. In fact, what you feel about marriage, I feel about mo-
> therhood, except that of the two relations motherhood seems to
> me the more destructive and limiting. But no doubt I'm merely
> trying to make out a case for myself. There's some truth in it,
> though. I don't like profound instincts—not in human relation-
> ships.[13]

Moving in the other direction of judgment, there are poignant moments that parallel the grief the young Virginia Stephen felt after her
father's lingering death from cancer in 1904. On March 5 of that year,
while she was assisting F. W. Maitland in his biography of Leslie Stephen by going over some of her father's letters, she wrote Violet
Dickinson:

> All this stupid writing and reading about Father seems to put him
> farther away only I know nothing can ever do that and I have the
> curious feeling of living with him every day. I often wonder as we
> sit talking what it is I am waiting for and then I know—I want to
> hear what he thinks. A most exquisite feeling to be with him, even
> to touch his hand—he was so quick and that one finds in no one
> else.[14]

And five days later she added:

> I know that it [father's death] wasn't really wrong; it had to be—
> but I can't bear to think of his loneliness and that I might have
> helped and didn't. If he had only lived I could have made up—I
> think he just knew how much I cared and the happy time was just
> beginning and now it is all over. That is what seems so cruel. If I
> could only tell him once—but it's no use writing it.[15]

Lily Briscoe, watching Mr. Ramsay sail away after she has rebuffed him, and suffering from the pain of "undischarged sympathy" is in the same plight.

But the triumph of the novel is not its truth as portrait. In searching to understand Mr. and Mrs. Ramsay, Virginia Woolf moved out of her obsessive memories and created both a psychic drama of her own divided self and a novel with the largeness of myth. Not only her parents, valued, comprehended, and forgiven; but her opposing selves, the feminine-intuitive and the masculine-analytic, are made living creatures.[16] In addition, the child Cam re-creates her child's-view of the past, and Lily Briscoe, who is in the end detached enough to abstract and fix the whole world of the novel, is an aspect of Virginia Woolf as well. Lily's rejection of the conventional sexual role Mrs. Ramsay urges on her is part of the exorcism. But most importantly for the power of the work, Mr. and Mrs. Ramsay, without losing their individual idiosyncracies, become archetypal figures.[17] "And suddenly the meaning which, for no reason at all, as perhaps they are stepping out of the Tube or ringing a doorbell, descends on people, making them symbolical, making them representative, came upon them, and made them in the dusk standing, looking the symbols of marriage, husband and wife" (pp. 110-111).

Virginia Woolf's comment on Conrad's later work may in part explain what she achieved in *To the Lighthouse:* "Conrad is not one and simple; no, he is many and complex, as we have often agreed. And it is when they simplify, when they reconcile their opposites—that they bring off (generally late in life) those complete books which for that reason we call their masterpieces."[18] *To the Lighthouse* makes possible an affirmative answer to Virginia Woolf's own question: "The novel, it is agreed, can follow life; it can amass details. But can it also select? Can it symbolize? It was some such function as this that poetry discharged in the past."[19]

A confident freedom with the facts marked the book's creation from the first; she altered the locale of her childhood holidays just as she changed biographical detail. The setting is the big, shabby summer home of the Ramsay family, overflowing with children and guests, isolated on an island in the Hebrides, dominated by the shape and the beam of the lighthouse, set far out to sea. The removal from Cornwall to the Hebrides she did not explain, but the flora and fauna of *To the Lighthouse* are not indigenous to that cold coast; comments on this anachronism caused her mild embarrassment when the book came out. That change, however, is not important. But the transformation of the house on the shore in St. Ives to the house on the microcosmic island, threatened by the sea, and the removal of the offshore Godrevy light to a misty and less accessible distance were imaginatively made for obvious symbolic and emotional reasons. This conceptual flexibility, her independence of both geographical fact and of consistently systematized symbolism as well, was characteristic of her imaginative freedom and power throughout the writing.

Her working notes from the beginning indicate the three sections of the novel's final form: "The Window," "Time Passes," and "The Lighthouse." "The Window" gradually and slowly develops the characters of the protagonists, beginning the search to understand them and to consider the large metaphysical problem of the relation of the self to others. Is this knowledge ever possible? The evidence about Mr. and Mrs. Ramsay is continually altered. She is maternal, gracious, intuitive, astonishingly beautiful, yet remote and subtly power-seeking. He is egocentric, self-pitying, tyrannical, emotionally dependent, yet admirably single-minded and disinterested in the pursuit of truth. Seventeen identifiable consciousnesses in the course of the novel play upon the questions of meaning and value that this relationship raises. The reader must be hypernaturally attuned to their biases.

The outer action of "The Window" revolves about a proposed trip to the lighthouse, an errand of kindness and a holiday excursion that bad weather threatens to postpone. Mrs. Ramsay encourages her youngest son, James, enthralled by her beauty and the security she provides, to hope for a fair day. Mr. Ramsay, believing this unrealistic opinion intolerably dishonest, destroys his son's anticipation by an accurate weather prediction of storm. James rages at his father's dominance and at his demands on Mrs. Ramsay's regenerative sympathy, pressures that deplete her creative powers. Guests observe and react to the Ramsays, revealing their own divided selves as well as offering conflicting points of view. The section climaxes with a dinner party celebrating an engagement that Mrs. Ramsay has fostered. Secretly and proudly exalted by her gift for harmonizing lives, she creates a temporary aura of peace and joy about the dinner table. "The Window" closes with a scene in which the couple alone acts out the interdependence and the silent conflict of their marriage.

The point of view is that of a general consciousness that encompasses minds related to each other through their senses and emotions, but rarely through their understandings. It is the imitation of a confluence of consciousnesses rather than the flow of separate streams, an indirect, third person technique perfectly designed to realize one of the novel's chief themes, the tenuous nature of human sympathy. It makes possible such a delicately balanced scene as the dinner party in which the whole occasion for all the threats of egotism and the angst of individual loneliness that work against its harmony, is momentarily suffused with a common joy.

The narrator's voice is so tentative, so questioning, that it merges almost undetected with the thoughts of the characters, sometimes taking over in mid-sentence. The ambiguity of its judgments and the limitations of its knowledge emphasize that human character cannot be finally summed up. The narrative voice creates what Virginia Woolf observed in the works of James, Dostoevsky, and Proust—"a deep reservoir of thought and emotion" developed by the brooding and analyzing voice of the author.[20] Its tone of melancholy doubt contrasts with the tone of nervous excitement pervading *Mrs. Dalloway,* an emotion that was perfectly suited to the rapidly alternating vignettes of a busy London day. The feelings of *To the Lighthouse* are like the slower rhythms of the sea; two kinds of emotion alternate like the tides. Both are typical of the quotidian life and of the search for perfected artistic creation: the deep quiet moments of achieved order and the frustrating interruptions of chaos—irritability, self-doubt, and egotistical anguish. By repeated images, whose highly subtle relationships the reader must detect, she builds up the climaxes until, as she wrote of De Quincey's method: "The emotion is never stated; it is suggested and brought slowly before us until it stays, in all its complexity, complete."[21]

In the short lyric central section, "Time Passes," natural imagery epitomizes the passage of time, the inexorable decay and destruction of nature, and the resilience and stubbornness of life. The fundamental relationship between the individual life, the individual death, and the processes of the universe is compressed symbolically into a few pages.

Parenthetically the death of Mrs. Ramsay, and the deaths of Andrew, in the war, and Prue, in a disease of pregnancy, are recorded. The family summer home mildews and crumbles. But a gallant, witless, and incorrigibly cheerful old charwoman, Mrs. McNab, readies it for the return of Mr. Ramsay, James, Cam, and Lily Briscoe, all changed by the sorrows of ten years.

In the final section, "The Lighthouse," life is placed in relation to art; the scene opens in disorder, conflict, and chaos. The children are cowed and coerced by their father, who insists on a memorial trip to the lighthouse, in part as a dramatization of his self-pitying grief. Lily senses that the occasion is portentous: "What does it mean, then, what can it all mean?" (p. 217). She longs to bring the fragmented feelings of all into a pattern that can discover significance; she tries to paint the picture that she composed in her mind ten years before at the dinner party.

The voyage is made at last. The simultaneous occurrence of three events evokes the single vision of the climax. Mr. Ramsay praises James' steering of the boat. Although his words are a particular approval, not the general blessing James craves, the son's jealous hatred of his father is temporarily allayed. James is able to see the lighthouse as the stark outline of his father's reasoned truth; earlier in the novel it had been the diffused golden light of his mother's sympathy. The two visions are at last unified.

Cam, after remembering old words of comfort from her mother's bedtime story, sees her father as a noble, lonely quester for truth, a triumphant hero and leader as he leaps onto the lighthouse rock.

The experience of Lily, painting on the lawn as the voyage is made, is more complex, for she brings the objectifying power of art to bear upon the scene and synthesizes it. Longing for the dead Mrs. Ramsay, Lily sees her apparition and is grateful, remembering her beauty and her power to make life stand still. But she also sternly and independently acknowledges Mrs. Ramsay's manipulations and errors of judgment. A sudden surge of sympathy allows Lily to forgive Mr. Ramsay his overbearing egotism and to admire his tenacious intellect. By the grace of Mrs. Ramsay's ghostly presence, and by her own power to see the strengths and weaknesses of both Mr. and Mrs. Ramsay, Lily achieves the necessary control, distance, and understanding, puts all the elements of this world into balance, and finishes her painting, putting a line in its center. All have experienced sympathy; all have felt the intensity of the search for insight. The lighthouse for a fleeting moment proves to be, not "one thing," but the points at which all positive values fuse.

No reading of the climactic vision can be offered without acknowledgment of the revisionist interpretations that have seen it as the total defeat of Mrs. Ramsay and the ultimate triumph of Mr. Ramsay. But to reverse completely the early angel-devil view of these two characters seems a dogmatic judgment that belies the psychological subtlety of the novel and ignores Virginia Woolf's persistent metaphor of balance. As Quentin Bell writes: "Virginia Woolf did not believe in angels or devils; or rather she believed in both but felt, and felt keenly, that they coexisted in the same persons."[22] The triumph of the last moment of the novel is that without any denial of their flaws, the strengths of Mr. and Mrs. Ramsay are put in the right relationship. That Mrs. Ramsay conceals or evades unpleasant truths does not cancel out her power to unify. That Mr. Ramsay is engaged in a lonely metaphysical quest on the periphery of knowledge does not negate the fact that he bullies his children. Lily does need to grow out of her uncritical worship of Mrs. Ramsay; she does need to bring her painting into harmony with Mr. Ramsay's ordered mind. But Mrs. Ramsay's ghostly return, both in Cam's involuntary memories and as the shadow that balances Lily's composition, is the catalyst that releases the resolving sympathy of the final vision.

The apotheosis is reached by the building up of minor details, fragmentary, confused, and contradictory experiences that defies arbitrary judgment but achieves at last a comprehensible unity. Virginia Woolf deliberately resisted working out rigid correspondences of meaning, concentrating on technical problems of composition, a kind of cubistic pattern, as Quentin Bell explains. This is not to say that the meanings of relationship are not there, but that she worked for emotional contrasts, not from a structure of ideas. Studying the novel one thinks of Lily Briscoe's explanation of her painting: "if there, in that corner, it was bright, here, in this, she felt the need of darkness " (p. 81). And Forster's comment on the color and shape of the novel seems more clear.

In answer to Roger Fry's inquiry about the "meaning" of the line that completed the picture, which he advanced diffidently and almost immediately withdrew, Virginia Woolf wrote: "I can't imagine symbolism except in a vague, generalized way, whether it's right or wrong, I don't know; but directly I'm told what a thing means it becomes hateful to me." And though Quentin Bell surmises she may have been a little flattering in the fullness of her emphasis, she went on to thank him for keeping her mind trained on problems of composition: "You have kept me on the right path so far as writing goes, more than anyone—if the right path it is."[23] Her attention to the relationship of "psychological volumes" contributed to her control of the disturbing material.

It is not surprising that the original working notes are once again primarily concerned with structural design. Yet they show, in contrast to those of *Mrs. Dalloway,* a greater concern for climactic scenes. It is clear why the *Lighthouse* moves in a more deliberate, measured, and periodic fashion. The first full working notes are dated August 6, 1925:

> The plan of the book is roughly that it should consist of three parts: one, Mrs. Ramsay (?) sitting at the window: while Mr. R. walks up and down in the dark: the idea being that there shall be curves of conversation or reflection or description or in fact anything, modulated by his appearance and disappearance at the window; gradually it shall grow calm; the child shall go to bed; the engaged couple shall appear; but this is all to be filled up as richly and variously as possible. My view being to find a unit for the sentence which shall be less emphatic and intense than that in Mrs. D., an everyday message for carrying on the narrative easily. The theme of the first part shall really contribute to Mrs. R.'s character: at least Mrs. R.'s character shall be displayed but finally in conjunction with his, so that one gets an impression of their relationship to propagate feeling; there shall be a time of waiting, of expectation. The child waiting to go to the lighthouse; the woman awaiting the return of the couple.
> (2) The passing of time: I am not sure how this is to be given: an interesting experiment, giving the sense of ten years passing.
> (3) This is the voyage to the Lighthouse. Several characters can be brought in: the young atheist. The old gentleman: the lovers: episodes can be written on woman's beauty: on truth: but these shall

be [one word illegible] and less knobbly than those in Mrs. D. making a more harmonious whole. There need be no specification of date. Whether this work be long or short, I do not know. The dominating impression is to be of Mr. R.'s character.[24]

The handwriting, always difficult to decipher, makes it near to impossible to distinguish between "Mr." and "Mrs." in the last line. Earlier notes had specified Mr. Ramsay as the dominating figure; it is possible that she is here reminding herself of this determination. But that Mrs. Ramsay's place in the first section is commanding cannot be denied; there was indeed a shift of emphasis, which Ruth Temple sees to be a loss of control.

One important indication of this early outline was carried out, however. The three parts of the novel stand in the same relations as to length as they do in the notes. This structure has sometimes been seen as A-B-A; pedantically it might be transcribed as A-b-$\frac{A}{2}$. The brevity of the final section has been regarded as a flaw. But the rationale of this plan seems perfectly harmonious with Virginia Woolf's theory of perspective and with her discussions of economy. The length of each section is harmonious with its elegiac action. The force that fights against death in "The Window" is the richness of the life of the mind that extends, expands, and deepens the moment, defeating clock time by the elasticity and range that it gives to experience. The Proustian blooming of the trivial events requires a long and fully developed section of the novel. In "Time Passes" the individual death is reduced by the cycle of the seasons and by the perennial resilience of "life itself" as epitomized by the incorrigibly cheerful Mrs. McNab. The sorrows of ten years pass in a night; the brevity of the section is in perfect harmony with the action and the theme.

It is, however, the length of "The Lighthouse" that has been considered a flaw in the design. Yet, remembering Virginia Woolf's praise of Ibsen's economy in limiting "the paraphernalia of reality" in moments when infinity is to be glimpsed may explain the compression of the final section. A chaos of unrelated passions is brought to life, developed from what James called "the ground of interest," created in the first section. Its elements are mastered and ordered. Art is the power that defies death in "The Lighthouse"; its technique of elegance and selectivity is perfectly appropriate. Virginia Woolf felt there was too much of artifice in the climax, but it was artifice that was central to the insight. And the seeming asymmetry of the whole may not have troubled her in a work which she said was influenced by Cézanne, whose architectonics successfully flouted conventional expectations of design.

To halt here in analyzing Virginia Woolf's theory and her novels is not to imply that *To the Lighthouse* brought about psychological and aesthetic liberation. After euphoria came depression; new variations of formal problems posed themselves in the work ahead. But there seems no denying that in *Mrs. Dalloway* and *To the Lighthouse* she had brilliantly achieved goals she had seen from the first and that she had explored in ways to which she was not to return the deepest questions raised by the giant figures towering over her childhood. She had worked from the beginning to make concrete and living the struggle between opposites, which was the inner life as she knew it; she had worked to control that tumult in a fictional form that would not limit its freedom and vitality. Lily Briscoe had described that balance: "Beautiful and bright it should be on the surface, feathery and evanescent, one colour melting into another like colours on a butterfly's wing: but beneath the fabric must be clamped together with bolts of iron" (p. 255).

That fabric was woven with light and dark threads, most closely gathered together in her late and private document, "A Sketch of the Past." There in the last years of her life she recorded her intense memories of early childhood. Describing her own talent as a writer as "shockability," she explained this as an awareness of the electric moments of being beneath the cotton-wool of mundane nonbeing.

Those moments, dark and bright, are the source, temperamental rather than intellectual, of the persistent shaping themes of her novels, of their tension, balance, and search. In "A Sketch of the Past" she brings to life insights of her early life: ecstasy in responding to the intermingled sights and sounds of St. Ives, fear and shame of her own body aroused by looking in the mirror, amusement at the odd humors of adults, paralysis at discovering the irrevocability of death, solace in life's unifying continuity, a sad futility in exchanging childish blows with her brother Thoby, and joy in understanding the globed wholeness of a plant and the earth from which it grew. Running through them all is the artist's pleasure in solidifying that which is ephemeral into an enduring substance.

Her power to make us feel these shocks of joy and grief makes the tribute that she wrote to another novelist a just one for herself:

> She possesses indisputably what seems to be as rare a gift as any— the gift of an entirely personal vision of life of which her books are the more or less complete embodiment. . . . She was completely and transparently faithful to her vision. In other words she was a true artist; and once we have said that of any writer we have to draw back a little and look at his work as a whole with the understanding that whether great art or lesser art, it is a thing unique of its kind.[25]

Few readers today would quarrel with the judgment that as Virginia Woolf learned to make that private vision more striking, piercing, and possessing, her work moved from the lesser to the greater realm of art.

Notes

Notes to chapter 1

1. "The Mark on the Wall," *A Haunted House and Other Stories,* p. 37.

2. *A Writer's Diary* (hereafter cited as *WD*), December 30, 1930, p. 160; July 27, 1934, p. 213. This is an edited edition of a personal diary kept by Virginia Woolf from 1915 until four days before her suicide by drowning in 1941. Leonard Woolf, her husband and its editor, describes the excerpts as "practically everything which referred to her own writing" (p. viii).

3. "How It Strikes A Contemporary," *Collected Essays* (hereafter cited as *CE*), vol. 2, pp. 158-159.

4. Review of *South Wind* by Norman Douglas, *Times Literary Supplement* (hereafter cited as *TLS*), June 15, 1917, p. 283.

5. "The Narrow Bridge of Art," *CE,* vol. 2, p. 228.

6. Review of *The Son of Royal Langbrith* by William Dean Howells, *The Guardian* (London), December 14, 1904, p. 2120.

7. Review of *Barham of Beltana* by W. E. Norris, *TLS,* March 14, 1905, p. 90.

8. Ibid.

9. *Virginia Woolf and Lytton Strachey: Letters*, p. 19.

10. Review of *Figures of Several Centuries* by Arthur Symons, *TLS*, December 21, 1916, p. 623.

11. "The Narrow Bridge of Art," *CE*, vol. 2, p. 228.

12. *WD*, November 18, 1924, pp. 67-68.

13. From an entry in Virginia Woolf's unpublished diary (April 14, 1918), quoted by Leonard Woolf in *Beginning Again*, p. 246. The date shows that she was referring to Joyce's unfinished manuscript, submitted to the Hogarth Press, and not to the published novel.

14. Letters from Virginia Woolf to Violet Dickinson spanning thirty-four years form part of the extensive archives of Woolf correspondence in the Henry W. and Albert A. Berg Collection of English and American Literature of The New York Public Library. The young Virginia Stephen wrote Miss Dickinson several times a week in the early years of their close friendship. This letter is dated May 18, 1919.

15. Review of *Madeleine, One of Love's Jansenists*, by Hope Mirrlees, *TLS*, October 9, 1919, p. 547.

16. "Phases of Fiction," *CE*, vol. 2, pp. 57, 100.

17. Ibid.

18. "On Re-reading Novels," *CE*, vol. 2, pp. 129-130.

19. Review of *Before Midnight* by Elinor Mordaunt, *TLS*, March 1, 1917, p. 104.

20. Letter to Vita Sackville-West quoted by Aileen Pippett in *The Moth and the Star* (New York: Viking, 1957), p. 220.

21. "Mr. Howells on Form," review of *The Actor Manager* by Leonard Merrick, *TLS*, November 15, 1918, p. 553.

22. "Oliver Goldsmith," *CE*, vol. 1, p. 110.

23. "A Letter to a Young Poet," *CE*, vol. 2, p. 184.

24. Dickinson correspondence, February 18, 1904, Berg Collection.

25. *WD*, October 2, 1932, p. 184. Yet Herbert Marder's *Feminism and Art: A Study of Virginia Woolf* quite properly makes the point that while "Virginia Woolf never succumbed to the temptation to turn the novel into a vehicle for propaganda, as did, for instance, D. H. Lawrence. On the other hand her novels are very far from being 'pure' works of art; there is, implicitly, a great deal of social criticism in them—a kind of latent propaganda" (p. 2).

26. Letter to Vanessa Bell, Wednesday, November 13, 1918, Berg Collection.

27. See S. P. Rosenbaum, "The Philosophical Realism of Virginia Woolf," *English Literature and British Philosophy*, pp. 316-356.

28. David Garnett, "Virginia Woolf," *The American Scholar*, vol. 34 (Summer 1965), p. 377.

29. Dickinson correspondence, dated only 1903, Berg Collection.

30. "An Unwritten Novel," *A Haunted House*, p. 15.

31. Dickinson correspondence, 1903, Berg Collection.

32. *WD*, December 8, 1929, p. 147. Her unpublished girlhood diary refers in

the August 9, 1897 entry to this project with self-mockery, calling it "the great work." Berg Collection.

33. Dickinson correspondence, 1903, Berg Collection.

34. Quentin Bell, *Virginia Woolf: A Biography*, vol. 1, p. 83.

35. E. M. Forster, *Virginia Woolf: The Rede Lecture*, p. 40.

36. "The Moment: Summer's Night," *CE*, vol. 2, p. 293.

37. *Night and Day*, p. 507. Hereafter page references will appear in the text.

38. See references to Virginia Woolf in Carolyn Heilbrun, *Toward a Recognition of Androgyny*.

39. Leonard Woolf, *The Journey Not the Arrival Matters: An Autobiography of the Years 1939-1969*, p. 73.

40. Review of *The Inward Light* by H. Fielding Hall, *TLS*, February 27, 1908, p. 68.

41. Forster, *Rede Lecture*, p. 27.

42. "Tchekov on Pope," unpublished typescript with author's manuscript corrections, Berg Collection.

Notes to chapter 2

1. "A Story to Make You Sleep," "Friendship's Gallery," Berg Collection. New York Public Library. "Written by Virginia Stephen and typed by her in 1907," is penciled on page 1 by Violet Dickinson.

2. Quotation from D. H. Lawrence's "Making Pictures" on flyleaf of *Paintings by D. H. Lawrence*, ed. Harry T. Moore, Jack Lindsay, and Herbert Read (New York, Viking Press, 1964).

3. "The Novels of George Gissing," *TLS*, January 3, 1912, p. 10.

4. "Phases of Fiction," *CE*, vol. 2, p. 101.

5. *Roger Fry, A Biography*, p. 239.

6. Quentin Bell, "The Life, Work, and Influence of Roger Fry," an introduction to the catalog for "An Exhibition arranged by the Arts Council and the University of Nottingham, 1966."

7. Jean Guiguet, *Virginia Woolf and Her Works*, pp. 154-155.

8. *WD*, June 23, 1920, p. 26.

9. *Roger Fry*, p. 240.

10. Dickinson correspondence, dated "Lane End, 1906," Berg Collection.

11. "Friendship's Gallery," p. 6, Berg Collection.

12. Ibid.

13. Roger Fry; *Letters of Roger Fry*, letter to Lady Fry, December 3, 1887, vol. 1, p. 118.

14. Compare this passage to that documented by note 3. Excerpt from Fry's "Sensibility," *Last Lectures*, p. 32:

> Now in works of art we find, I suspect, something like a compromise between the mathematical order in which the intellect finds satisfaction and the conformity to type, but with the infinite variation which distinguishes organic life. In art there is at once order and uniqueness, which means

incessant variation from the precise or mathematical order. . . . It is in this region then, which lies between rigid order and chaos that the artist's sensibility functions.

15. Roger Fry, "Some Questions in Aesthetics," *Transformations: Critical and Speculative Essays on Art,* p. 5. The following quotations and paraphrasing are from this essay.

16. Ibid., p. 9.

17. *Roger Fry,* pp. 239-240.

18. Fry, "Some Questions in Aesthetics," *Transformations,* p. 9.

19. Roger Fry, *The Artist and Psychoanalysis,* p. 19.

20. Fry, "Some Questions in Aesthetics," *Transformations,* p. 9.

21. "The Art of Fiction," *CE,* vol. 2, pp. 54-55. Forster replied to this in a letter, asking: "And why do you complain that no critic in England will judge the novel as a work of art? Percy Lubbock does nothing else. Yet he does not altogether satisfy you. Why?" E. M. Forster to Virginia Woolf, November 7, 1928, Berg Collection.

22. E. M. Forster, *Aspects of the Novel,* p. 80.

23. "The Novels of E. M. Forster," *CE,* vol. 1, pp. 342-351.

24. Ibid., pp. 344-345.

25. Ibid., p. 346.

26. Ibid., p. 351.

27. E. M. Forster to Virginia Woolf, November 7, 1928, Berg Collection.

28. Ibid.

29. E. M. Forster to Virginia Woolf, October 16, 1927, Berg Collection.

30. E. M. Forster, *Virginia Woolf: The Rede Lecture,* p. 22.

31. Forster, *Aspects of the Novel,* p. 163.

32. Henry James, "The Art of Fiction," *Theory of Fiction: Henry James,* edited with an introduction by James E. Miller, Jr. (Lincoln: University of Nebraska Press, 1971), p. 35.

33. "Mr. Henry James' Latest Novel," review of *The Golden Bowl, The Guardian* [London], February 22, 1905, p. 339.

34. Ibid.

35. "The Method of Henry James," *TLS,* December 26, 1918, p. 655.

36. "Henry James' Ghost Stories," *TLS,* December 22, 1921, p. 850.

37. Virginia Woolf to Vanessa Bell, November 11, 1918, Berg Collection.

38. Leonard Woolf, *Sowing: An Autobiography of the Years 1880-1904,* p. 120.

39. Ibid.

40. Dickinson correspondence, August 27, 1907, Berg Collection.

41. *Virginia Woolf and Lytton Strachey: Letters,* October 22, 1915, p. 70.

42. Letter to William Dean Howells, January 31, 1880, *The Letters of Henry James,* ed. Percy Lubbock (New York: Scribner, 1920), vol. 1, p. 72.

43. "American Fiction," *CE,* vol. 2, p. 119.

44. Review of *The Letters of Henry James, CE,* vol. 2, p. 284; "American Fiction," *CE,* vol. 2, p. 119.

45. "The Method of Henry James."

46. *WD*, September 12, 1921, p. 39.

47. Henry James' preface to *The Awkward Age* as quoted by Virginia Woolf in her review, "The Method of Henry James."

48. "Modern Fiction," *CE*, vol. 2, p. 106.

49. *To the Lighthouse* (New York, 1927), p. 240.

50. Virginia Woolf to Roger Fry, August 29, 1921, Monks House Papers.

51. "Phases of Fiction," *CE*, vol. 2, p. 82.

52. "On Re-reading Novels," *CE*, vol. 2, p. 128.

53. "Mr. Henry James' Latest Novel."

54. Preface to "The Author of Beltraffo," (New York, 1909).

55. "Mr. Henry James' Latest Novel."

56. "Phases of Fiction," *CE*, vol. 2, p. 81.

57. Review of *The Park Wall* by Elinor Mordaunt, *TLS*, August 31, 1916, p. 415.

58. "Mr. Symon's Essays," a review of *Figures of Several Centuries* by Arthur Symons, *TLS*, December 21, 1916, p. 623.

Notes to chapter 3

1. All quotations in this paragraph are from "Mr. Symons' Essays," *TLS*, December 21, 1916, p. 623.

2. "Patmore's Criticism," *TLS*, May 26, 1921, p. 331.

3. Ibid.

4. "Creative Criticism," *TLS*, June 8, 1917, p. 271.

5. Charles Augustin Sainte-Beuve as translated by Walter Bate in the introduction to "What Is a Classic?" in *Criticism: the Major Texts*, ed. Walter Jackson Bate (New York: Harcourt, Brace and World, 1952), p. 490.

6. "David Copperfield," *CE*, vol. 1, p. 192.

7. "George Gissing," *CE*, vol. 1, p. 297.

8. "The Novels of Thomas Hardy," *CE*, vol. 1, p. 257; "David Copperfield," *CE*, vol. 2, p. 193; "De Quincey's Autobiography," *CE*, vol. 4, p. 5.

9. "Sterne," *CE*, vol. 3, p. 86.

10. *"Robinson Crusoe," CE,* vol. 1, p. 70.

11. "Phases of Fiction," *CE*, vol. 2, p. 90.

12. Ibid.; "The Novels of Thomas Hardy," *CE*, vol. 1, p. 262.

13. "The Novels of E. M. Forster," *CE*, vol. 1, p. 351.

14. *WD*, May 9, 1935, p. 239.

15. "Notes on an Elizabethan Play," *CE*, vol. 1, p. 54.

16. "On Not Knowing Greek," *CE*, vol. 1, p. 3.

17. "Joseph Conrad," *CE*, vol. 1, p. 307.

18. "Modern Fiction," *CE*, vol. 2, p. 108.

19. "William Hazlitt," *CE*, vol. 1, p. 163.

20. "Edmund Gosse," *CE*, vol. 4, p. 86.

21. "Creative Criticism," *TLS*, June 8, 1917, p. 271.

22. Ibid.

Notes   149

23. Virginia Woolf as quoted by Jean Guiguet in the preface to *Contemporary Writers*, p. 11.

24. "The Claim of the Living," *TLS*, June 13, 1918, p. 275.

25. "The Green Mirror," *TLS*, January 24, 1918, p. 43.

26. "A Character Sketch," *Athenaeum*, August 13, 1920, pp. 201-202.

27. Dickinson correspondence, November, 1907, Berg Collection.

28. *Jacob's Room* (New York, 1923), p. 70. Hereafter page references will be cited in the text.

29. "The Pursuit of Beauty," review of *Linda Condon* by Joseph Hergesheimer, *TLS*, July 8, 1920, p. 437.

30. *WD*, May 6, 1935, p. 239.

31. "A Man with a View," *TLS*, July 20, 1916, p. 343.

32. "The Rights of Youth," a review of *Joan and Peter* by H. G. Wells, *TLS*, September 19, 1918, p. 439.

33. Ibid.

34. "The Green Mirror."

35. Review of *Mummery* by Gilbert Cannan, *TLS*, December 19, 1918, p. 641.

36. "Freudian Fiction." The question of why Virginia Woolf never submitted to psychoanalysis has been raised. Quentin Bell explains that at the time of her critical mental illness it was against professional ethics for a psychiatrist to treat a patient who had exhibited signs of madness. Later "she showed little interest and less enthusiasm for the discoveries of Freud and could not have been persuaded to consult a psychiatrist." Quentin Bell, *Virginia Woolf: A Biography*, vol. 2, pp. 19-20n. Freud's view that a woman could not have a creative mind would surely have raised her ire.

37. "The Modern Essay," *CE*, vol. 2, p. 50; *WD*, October 2, 1932, p. 183.

Notes to chapter 4

1. "How Should One Read a Book?" *CE*, vol. 2, p. 1.

2. "Gas," *CE*, vol. 2, pp. 298-299.

3. Review of *The Mills of the Gods* by Elizabeth Robins, *TLS*, June 18, 1920, p. 383.

4. "The Intellectual Imagination," *TLS*, December 11, 1919, p. 739.

5. *WD*, January 26, 1920, p. 22.

6. Holograph working notes, Berg Collection.

7. Ibid.

8. *WD*, July 20, 1925, p. 79.

9. Holograph working notes, Berg Collection.

10. *WD*, May 22, 1934, pp. 211-212.

11. *WD*, November 28, 1928, p. 136.

12. Leonard Woolf, *Beginning Again: An Autobiography of the Years 1911-1918*, p. 232.

13. *WD*, February 7, 1931, p. 165.
14. John Lehmann, "Working with Virginia Woolf," p. 62.
15. *WD*, May 11, 1920, p. 25.
16. "Phases of Fiction," *CE*, vol. 2, p. 70.
17. *WD*, July 20, 1925, p. 79.
18. *WD*, June 19, 1923, p. 56.
19. Letter to Charles Percy Sanger quoted by Dorothy Brewster in *Virginia Woolf*, p. 163.
20. *WD*, January 6, 1925, p. 70.
21. Quentin Bell, "The Biographer, The Critic and the Lighthouse," *Ariel*, January 1971, vol. 2, pp. 94-101.
22. *WD*, May 25, 1926, p. 88.
23. Holograph manuscript, Berg Collection.
24. "Phases of Fiction," *CE*, vol. 2, p. 77.
25. E. M. Forster, "The Early Novels of Virginia Woolf," pp. 106-115.
26. "The Lady in the Looking Glass," *A Haunted House*, pp. 80-81.

Notes to chapter 5

1. *Mrs. Dalloway* (London, 1954), p. 5. All subsequent quotations are to the edition cited.
2. Holograph working notes, October 16, 1922, Berg Collection.
3. *WD*, August 15, 1924, p. 64.
4. Quentin Bell, *Virginia Woolf: A Biography*, vol. 2, Appendix D, "Clive Bell and the Writing of *The Voyage Out*," Letter, Virginia Stephen to Clive Bell, February 7, 1909, p. 211.
5. Ibid., Clive Bell to Virginia Stephen, October 1908, p. 208.
6. Leonard Woolf, *Beginning Again: An Autobiography of the Years 1911-1918* p. 88.
7. Clive Bell, "Virginia Woolf," *Dial* 77 (December 1924): 456.
8. David Daiches, *Virginia Woolf* (Norfolk, Connecticut: New Directions, 1942), p. 16.
9. Jean Guiguet, *Virginia Woolf and Her Works*, p. 197; A. P. Moody, *Virginia Woolf* (New York, 1963), p. 11.
10. James Hafley, *The Glass Roof; Virginia Woolf as Novelist*, p. 26.
11. Bell, *Virginia Woolf*, Appendix D, Clive Bell to Virginia Stephen, February, 1909, p. 210.
12. Dickinson correspondence, January 11, 1909, dated in the handwriting of Violet Dickinson, Berg Collection. Quentin Bell, correcting my transcription of the word "graves" to "groves," suggests that the incident may have occurred in Greece where the two friends toured together.
13. J. Thomas to Violet Dickinson, September 14, 1913, Dickinson correspondence, Berg Collection.

14. *WD,* March 27, 1919, p. 11.
15. "The Patron and the Crocus," *CE,* vol. 2, p. 151.
16. Ibid.
17. Bell, *Virginia Woolf,* Appendix D, Clive Bell to Virginia Stephen, February 1909, p. 209.
18. For this linguistic analysis I am indebted to Elizabeth McKee Eddy, "A Study of the Style of Mrs. Virginia Woolf with Special Emphasis on Her Thought Patterns" (Master's thesis, University of Chicago, 1930).
19. Earlier typescript, *The Voyage Out,* incomplete, with the author's manuscript corrections, unsigned and undated, Berg Collection.
20. Leonard Woolf, *Beginning Again,* p. 79.
21. Early typescript, Berg Collection.
22. From a notebook labeled "Essays, 1940." Diary for October 12 says "Scraps of memoirs come so coolingly to my mind." Berg Collection.
23. *Woolf-Strachey Letters,* February 25, 1916, p. 73.
24. Ibid, p. 75.
25. *WD,* January 5, 1933, p. 187.
26. *WD,* March 27, 1919, p. 10.
27. *Night and Day,* (New York, 1920), p. 313.

Notes to chapter 6

1. Holograph working notes, "Jacob's Room," dated April 15, 1920, Berg Collection.
2. See S. P. Rosenbaum, "The Philosophical Realism of Virginia Woolf," *English Literature and British Philosophy,* pp. 328-331, for a full exploration of this question.
3. "Sterne," *CE,* vol. 3, p. 90.
4. Leonard Woolf, *Downhill All the Way* (London: Hogarth Press, 1967), p. 59.
5. *WD,* April 8, 1925, p. 71.
6. Letter to Roger Fry, "Saturday" [1922], Monks House Papers.
7. "More Dostoevsky," *TLS,* February 23, 1917, p. 91.
8. Ibid.
9. In a detailed discussion of his wife's most serious illness, Leonard Woolf says: "In all these cases of breakdown there were two distinct stages which are technically called manic-depressive." *Beginning Again* (New York, 1964), p. 76. Dr. Charles Brenner describes the conspicuous thought pattern of the manic-depressive patient as "primary process thinking" and characterizes it thus: "In primary process thinking representation by allusion or allegory is frequent and a part of an object, memory, or idea may be used to stand for the whole or vice versa. Moreover, several different thoughts may be represented by a single thought or image. In fact, verbal representation is not used nearly as exclusively in primary

as in secondary process thinking. Visual or other sense impressions may appear instead of a word, or for that matter instead of a paragraph or a whole chapter of words. As a final characteristic we may add that a sense of time, or a concern with time does not exist in primary process thinking." Charles Brenner, *An Elementary Textbook of Psychoanalysis* (Garden City: Doubleday and Co., 1955), pp. 53-54.

10. *WD*, September 10, 1929, p. 143.

11. Jean Guiguet, preface, in Virginia Woolf, *Contemporary Writers*, p. 62.

12. Letter to Vanessa Bell, "Monday, 1918," Berg Collection.

13. Sergei Eisenstein, "The Cinematographic Principle and the Ideogram," *Film Form*, translated by Jay Leda (New York: Harcourt, Brace and Co., 1949), pp. 34-35. Originally published as an afterword entitled "Outside the Frame," in Nikolai Kaufman's brochure, *Japanese Cinema* (Moscow, 1929). Other striking similarities between the technique of film making and Virginia Woolf's literary technique are made clear as Eisenstein discusses the means by which film montage includes the mind of the viewer in the creative process of the reader or viewer. The viewer "experiences the dynamic process of the emergence and assembly of the image just as it was experienced by the author."

14. Holograph working notes, August 6, 1925, Berg Collection.

15. Eisenstein, *"Cinematographic Principle."*

16. Ibid.

17. *WD*, January 26, 1920, p. 22. "Conceive (?) *Mark on the Wall, K. G.,* and *Unwritten Novel* taking hands and dancing in unity." "Suppose one thing should open out of another—as in an unwritten novel—only not for 10 pages but 200 or so—doesn't that give the looseness and lightness I want; doesn't that get closer and yet keep form and speed, and enclose everything, everything?"

18. Carolyn G. Heilbrun, *Toward a Recognition of Androgyny*, p. 164.

19. "Phases of Fiction," *CE*, vol. 2, p. 94.

20. "A Glance at Turgenev," *TLS*, December 8, 1921, p. 813.

21. *Woolf-Strachey Letters*, October 9, 1922, p. 144.

22. Lytton Strachey letter quoted by Michael Holroyd, *Lytton Strachey* (New York: Holt, Rinehart and Winston, 1968), p. 107.

23. *WD*, February 7, 1931, p. 165.

24. Quentin Bell, *Virginia Woolf, A Biography*, vol. 1, p. 112.

25. Dickinson correspondence, December 22, 1906, Berg Collection.

26. Ibid., November 20, 1906.

27. Ibid., November 26, 1906.

28. Ibid., December 19, 1906.

29. E. M. Forster, "The Early Novels of Virginia Woolf," *Abinger Harvest*, p. 110.

30. A letter to Charles Percy Sanger, dated October 30, 1922, quoted by Dorothy Brewster in *Virginia Woolf*, pp. 162-163.

31. *Woolf-Strachey Letters*, October 9, 1922, p. 144.

32. Ibid., October 9 10th?, 1922, p. 146.

33. *Roger Fry*, p. 241.

34. *WD*, March 27, 1919, p. 10.

Notes 153

35. "Most of life is so dull that there is nothing to be said about it, and the books and talk that would describe it are obliged to exaggerate, in the hope of justifying their own existence. Inside its cocoon of work or social obligation, the human spirit slumbers for the most part, registering the distinction between pleasure and pain, but not nearly so alert as we pretend. There are periods in the most thrilling day during which nothing happens . . . and a perfectly adjusted organism would be silent." E. M. Forster, *A Passage to India* (New York: Harcourt, Brace and World, 1924), pp. 132-133.

Notes to chapter 7

1. *WD,* December 13, 1924, p. 68.
2. Introduction to *Mrs. Dalloway* (New York, 1925), p. viii.
3. *WD,* September 26, 1920, p. 27.
4. *WD,* October 29, 1922, p. 53.
5. *WD,* September 25, 1925, pp. 80-81.
6. Introduction to *Mrs. Dalloway* (New York, 1925), p. viii.
7. *WD,* June 19, 1923, p. 56.
8. "Professions for Women," *CE,* vol. 2, p. 287.
9. Holograph working notes, Berg Collection.
10. "The notes for a revision of the novel reveal the shift in focus from external political and social concerns to internal perspectives." Charles G. Hoffmann, "From Short Story to Novel: The Manuscript Revisions of Virginia Woolf's *Mrs. Dalloway,*" *Modern Fiction Studies* 2:176.
11. Introduction to *Mrs. Dalloway,* Modern Library edition, p. vi. Kitty Maxse, who Virginia Woolf says in her diary was the model for Clarissa, died of a fall resulting from a faint on October 6.
12. Dickinson correspondence, letter dated only "1903," Berg Collection.
13. Holograph notebook, June 18, 1923, Berg Collection.
14. Holograph notebook, Berg Collection.
15. "Mrs. Dalloway on Bond Street," *Dial* 75: (July, 1923): 20-27. Subsequent quotations from the story will be documented in the text.
16. *WD,* September 7, 1924, p. 65.
17. See volume 2 of Quentin Bell's *Virginia Woolf: A Biography* for full discussion.
18. *WD,* October 15, 1923, p. 60.
19. *WD,* September 7, 1924, p. 66.
20. "The Cinematographic Principle and the Ideogram," abridged from *Film Form* by Sergei Eisenstein, ed. and trans. Jay Leyda (New York, 1949) as it appears in *The Essential Prose,* ed. Dorothy Van Ghent and Willard Mass (New York: Bobbs-Merrill Co., 1966), p. 730.
21. "Across the Border," review of *The Supernatural in Modern English Fiction,* by Dorothy Scarborough, *TLS,* February 1, 1918, p. 55.
22. *WD,* June 19, 1923, p. 56.

23. Entry in notebook, dated November 9, 1922, Berg Collection.

24. Dickinson correspondence, October 30, 1904, Berg Collection.

25. *WD*, June 18, 1925, pp. 77-78.

26. Jacqueline Latham, "The Model for Clarissa Dalloway-Kitty Maxse," *Notes and Queries*, pp. 262-263. Mrs. Maxse is further discussed in the Bell biography.

27. A. D. Moody, *Virginia Woolf*, p. 19.

28. *WD*, June 18, 1925, p. 77.

29. *WD*, July 30, 1925, p. 80.

Notes to chapter 8

1. *WD*, November 23, 1926, p. 101; September 5, 1926, p. 98.

2. *WD*, February 23, 1926, p. 84.

3. *WD*, November 23, 1926, p. 101.

4. E. M. Forster to Virginia Woolf, June 5, 1926, Berg Collection.

5. Leonard Woolf, foreword to Mitchell Leaska, *Virginia Woolf's Lighthouse: A Study in Critical Method*, pp. 11-12.

6. Ruth Z. Temple, "Never Say 'I': *To the Lighthouse* as Vision and Confession," in *Virginia Woolf: A Collection of Critical Essays*, ed. Claire Sprague, pp. 90-100.

7. Mitchell Leaska, *Virginia Woolf's Lighthouse: A Study in Critical Method*.

8. *WD*, November 28, 1929, p. 135.

9. Virginia Woolf to Vanessa Bell, May 22, 1927, Berg Collection.

10. Virginia Woolf to Vanessa Bell, May 25, 1927, Berg Collection.

11. "Friendship's Gallery," pp. 15-16, Berg Collection.

12. Early typescript, "The Voyage Out," Berg Collection.

13. Virginia Woolf to Vanessa Bell, May 22, 1927, Berg Collection.

14. Virginia Stephen to Violet Dickinson, March 5, 1904 (the year of Leslie Stephen's death), Berg Collection.

15. Virginia Stephen to Violet Dickinson, March 10, 1904, Berg Collection.

16. See Nancy Topping Bazin, "Virginia Woolf's Quest for Equilibrium," *Modern Language Quarterly*, vol. 32, no. 3 (September 1971), from which this observation and terminology are drawn.

17. See Joseph Blotner, "Mythic Patterns in *To the Lighthouse*."

18. "Mr. Conrad: A Conversation," *CE*, vol. 1, p. 310. First published, 1923.

19. "Phases of Fiction," *CE*, vol. 2, p. 102.

20. "Phases of Fiction," *CE*, vol. 2, p. 88.

21. "De Quincey's Autobiography," *CE*, vol. 4, p. 2.

22. Quentin Bell, "The Biographer, The Critic, and *The Lighthouse*," *Ariel*, January 1971, vol. 2, pp. 1, 100-101.

23. Virginia Woolf to Roger Fry, May 27, 1927, as quoted by Quentin Bell, ibid.

24. Holograph working notes, entry dated August 6, 1925, Berg Collection.

25. "Lady Ritchie," *TLS,* March 6, 1919, p. 123. Thackeray's daughter, Virginia Woolf's aunt, sister of Leslie Stephen's first wife.

Bibliography

Works by Virginia Woolf

Fiction and collected essays

Between the Acts. London: Hogarth Press, 1941.

The Captain's Death Bed and Other Essays. London: Hogarth Press, 1950.

Collected Essays. 4 volumes. New York: Harcourt, Brace and World, 1966.

The Common Reader. New York: Harcourt, Brace, 1925.

The Common Reader. Second Series. London: Hogarth Press, 1948. First published 1932.

Contemporary Writers. Edited by Jean Guiguet. London: Hogarth Press, 1965.

The Death of the Moth and Other Essays. New York: Harcourt, Brace, 1942.

Flush: A Biography. London: Hogarth Press, 1933.

Granite and Rainbow. London: Hogarth Press, 1958.

A Haunted House and Other Stories. London: Hogarth Press, 1944. First published 1943.

Jacob's Room. New York: Harcourt, Brace, and World, 1950. First published 1922.

The Moment and Other Essays. London: Hogarth Press, 1952. First published 1947.

Monday or Tuesday. New York: Harcourt, Brace, 1921.

Mrs. Dalloway. London: Hogarth Press, 1954. First published 1925.

Night and Day. New York: Harcourt, Brace, 1920. First published 1919.

Orlando: A Biography. New York: Harcourt, Brace, 1928.

Roger Fry: A Biography. London: Hogarth Press, 1940.

A Room of One's Own. New York: Harcourt, Brace, 1929.

Three Guineas. London: Hogarth Press, 1958. First published 1932.

To the Lighthouse. New York: Harcourt, Brace and World, 1955. First published 1927.

The Voyage Out. New York: George H. Doran Co., 1920. First published 1915.

The Waves. London: Hogarth Press, 1955. First published 1931.

A Writer's Diary. Edited by Leonard Woolf. New York: Harcourt, Brace and Company, 1953.

The Years. New York: Harcourt, Brace, 1937.

Virginia Woolf and Lytton Strachey: Letters. Edited by Leonard Woolf and James Strachey. New York: Harcourt, Brace, 1956.

Reviews and articles cited

"Across the Border." Review of *The Supernatural in Modern English Fiction* by Dorothy Scarborough, *TLS,* February 1, 1915, p. 55.

"American Fiction." *Saturday Review of Literature* 2 (August 1, 1925–: 1-3.

"Barham of Beltana." Review of *Barham of Beltana* by William Norris, *TLS,* March 14, 1905, p. 90.

"Before Midnight." Review of *Before Midnight* by Elinor Mordaunt, *TLS,* March 1, 1917, p. 104.

"A Character Sketch." Review of Frederick Locker-Lampson: *A Character Sketch,* edited by Augustine Birrell, *Athenaeum,* August 13, 1920, pp. 201-202.

"The Claim of the Living." Review of *A Novelist on Novels* by W. L. George, *TLS,* June 13, 1918, p. 275.

"Creative Criticism." Review of *Creative Criticism: Essays on The Unity of Genius and Taste,* by J. E. Spingarn, *TLS,* June 8, 1917, p. 271.

"David Copperfield." *Nation & Athenaeum,* August 22, 1925, pp. 620-621.

"De Quincey's Autobiography." First published in *The Common Reader: Second Series.* London: Hogarth Press, 1932.

"Edmund Gosse." *Fortnightly Review,* June 1, 1931, pp. 766-773.

"The Faery Queen." First published in *The Moment and other Essays.* London: Hogarth Press, 1947.

"Freudian Fiction." Review of *An Imperfect Mother,* by J. D. Beresford, *TLS,* March 26, 1920, p. 199.

"A Glance at Turgenev." Review of *The Two Friends and Other Stories,* translated by Constance Garnett. *TLS,* December 8, 1921, p. 813.

"George Gissing." *Nation & Athenaeum*, February 26, 1927, pp. 722-723.

"The Green Mirror." Review of *The Green Mirror*, by Hugh Walpole, *TLS*, January 24, 1918, p. 43.

"Honest Fiction." Review of *Shops and Houses*, by Frank Swinnerton, *TLS*, October 10, 1918, p. 481.

"How Should One Read a Book?" *Yale Review* 16 (October, 1926): 32-44.

"How It Strikes A Contemporary." *TLS*, April 5, 1923, pp. 221-222.

"The Intellectual Imagination." Review of Rupert Brooke and *The Intellectual Imagination: A Lecture*, by Walter de la Mare, *TLS*, December 11, 1919, p. 739.

Introduction, *Mrs. Dalloway*. New York: Modern Library, 1928.

"The Inward Light." Review of *The Inward Light* by H. Fielding Hall, *TLS*, February 27, 1908, p. 68.

"Lady Ritchie." *TLS*, March 6, 1919, p. 123.

"The Leaning Tower." A paper read to the Workers' Educational Association, Brighton, May 1940, published in *Collected Essays*, vol. 2, pp. 162-181.

"A Letter to a Young Poet." *Yale Review* 21 (June 1932): 696-710.

"The Letters of Henry James." Review of *The Letters of Henry James*, edited by Percy Lubbock. *TLS*, April 8, 1920, pp. 217-218.

"Madeleine." Review of *Madeleine, One of Love's Jansenists*, by Hope Mirrlees. *TLS*, October 9, 1919, p. 547.

"A Man with a View." Review of *Samuel Butler: Author of Erewhon, the Man and His Work*, by John F. Harris, *TLS*, July 20, 1916.

"The Method of Henry James." Review of *The Method of Henry James*, by Joseph Warren Beach. *TLS*, December 26, 1918, p. 655.

"The Mills of the Gods." Review of *The Mills of the Gods* by Elizabeth Robins, *TLS*, June 18, 1920, p. 383.

"The Moment." First published in *The Moment and Other Essays*. London: Hogarth Press, 1947.

"Mr. Bennett and Mrs. Brown." *Literary Review of the New York Evening Post*, November 17, 1923, pp. 253-254.

"Mr. Henry James' Latest Novel." Review of *The Golden Bowl*. *The Guardian* (London), February 22, 1905, p. 339.

"Mr. Howells on Form." Review of *The Actor Manager*, by Leonard Merrick. *TLS*, November 15, 1918, p. 553.

"Mr. Symons' Essays." Review of *Figures of Several Centuries*, by Arthur Symons, *TLS*, December 21, 1916, p. 623.

"Mrs. Gaskell." Review of *Mrs. Gaskell: Haunts, Homes and Stories*, by Mrs. Ellis H. Chadwick, *TLS*, September 29, 1910, p. 349.

"Modern Novels." *TLS*, April 10, 1919, pp. 189-190. Reprinted (slightly revised) as "Modern Fiction" in *Collected Essays*.

"More Dostoevsky." Review of *The Eternal Husband and Other Stories*, by Fyodor Dostoevsky, translated by Constance Garnett. *TLS*, February 23, 1917, p. 91.

"Mummery." Review of *Mummery* by Gilbert Cannan, *TLS*, December 18, 1918, p. 641.

"The Narrow Bridge of Art." Published as "Poetry, Fiction, and the Future."
   New York Herald Tribune, August 14, 1927, section 7, books 1, 6-7; and
   August 21, 1927, section 6, books 1, 6.
"The Novels of E. M. Forster." *Atlantic Monthly,* November 1927, pp. 642-648.
"The Novels of George Gissing." *TLS,* January 1912, pp. 9-10.
"The Old Order." Review of *The Middle Years,* by Henry James. *TLS,* October
   19, 1917, pp. 497-498.
"Oliver Goldsmith." *TLS,* March 1, 1934, pp. 133-134.
"On Being Ill." *New Criterion* 4 (January 1926):32-45.
"On Not Knowing Greek." First published in *The Common Reader.* London:
   Hogarth Press, 1925.
"The Park Wall." Review of *The Park Wall* by Elinor Mordaunt, *TLS,* August 31,
   1916, p. 415.
"Patmore's Criticism." Review of *Courage in Politics and Other Essays,* by Coven-
   try Patmore. *TLS,* May 26, 1921, p. 331.
"The Patron and the Crocus." *Nation & Athenaeum,* April 12, 1924, pp. 46-47.
"Pursuit of Beauty." Review of *Linda Condon* by Joseph Hergesheimer, *TLS,*
   July 8, 1920, p. 437.
"The Rights of Youth." A review of *Joan and Peter* by H. G. Wells, *TLS,* Sep-
   tember 19, 1918, p. 439.
"Romance and the Heart." Review of *Revolving Lights,* by Dorothy Richardson.
   Nation & Athenaeum, May 1923, p. 229.
"A Room with a View." Review of *Room with a View,* by E. M. Forster. *TLS,*
   October 22, 1908, p. 362.
"Scott's Character." Review of *The Intimate Life of Sir Walter Scott* by Archi-
   bald Stalker. *TLS,* April 28, 1921, p. 273.
"South Wind." Review of *South Wind* by Norman Douglas, *TLS,* June 15, 1917,
   p. 283.
"William Hazlitt, the Man." *New York Herald Tribune,* September 7, 1930, sec-
   tion 11, books 1, 4. Review of *The Complete Works of William Hazlitt,* edited
   by P. P. Howe, vols. 1, 4, and 5.

Archival material examined

Cambridge, Kings College Library. Charleston Papers. Papers inherited by
   Angelica Garnett and Quentin Bell. Letters and Papers of Duncan Grant. Papers
   of E. M. Forster.
Palmer, Brighton. Documents Section, University of Sussex Library.
   Monks House Papers:
      Correspondence between Leonard and Virginia Woolf, 1912-1936.
      Letters to and from Leonard Woolf, 1913-1947.
      Letters to and from Virginia Woolf, 1912-1941.
      Juvenilia, reminiscences of family and childhood, early travel journals,
      typescript drafts, fragments, reading notes, Memoir Club Contributions,

report on teaching at Morley College, unpublished complete stories and sketches, unpublished essays, holograph manuscripts.

London. British Museum. "Mrs. Dalloway" holograph manuscript.

New York. Henry W. and Albert A. Berg Collection, the New York Public Library, Astor, Lenox and Tilden Foundations. Twenty-seven volumes of diary by Virginia Woolf, 1915-1941. (Two volumes for 1918, none for 1916.)

Eight holograph notebooks recording the following periods: January 1897 - January 1898; August - September 1899; June - October 1903; December 1904 - May 1905; August - September 1905; April 1906 - August 1908; August - October 1918; September - October 1919.

Ten volumes of notebooks containing articles, essays, fiction, and reviews written during the years 1925-1940.

Archival material cited or referred to in the text

New York. Henry W. and Albert A. Berg Collection, the New York Public Library, Astor, Lenox and Tilden Foundations.

"Ancestors." Holograph beginning of story featuring Mrs. Dalloway. May 18, 1925. 3 pp.

Correspondence with E. M. Forster.

Correspondence with Vanessa Bell.

Correspondence with Violet Dickinson, 1902-1936.

Diary. Bound notebook dated January 1, 1898.

"Friendship's Gallery." Typescript with corrections in the author's and unidentified hands. 52 pp. Includes "A Story to Make You Sleep."

"Incongruous Memories." Holograph. Undated. 5 pp.

"The Introduction." Holograph story featuring Mrs. Dalloway. Undated. 9 pp.

"Jacob's Room." Holograph notebooks.

Part 1. April 15, 1920 - November 24, 1920. 109 pp.

Part 2. Hogarth house, Richmond, November 26, 1920 - May 6, 1921. 130 pp.

Part 3. March 12, 1922. 23 pp. This notebook includes the first version of "The Hours."

"Jacob's Room." Typescript of Chapter 10, with author's manuscript corrections. Undated. 6 pp. Not included in published version.

"Mrs. Dalloway."

Holograph outline entitled "At home; or the party." October 6, 1922. 1 p.

"A possible revision of this book." Holograph notes. October 16, 1922. 1 p. In Part 3 of holograph manuscript of "Jacob's Room."

"The Prime Minister." In Part 3 of "Jacob's Room" holograph.

"Tchekov on Pope." Typescript.

Part 1. Monk's House, August 6, 1925 - March 16, 1927. 167 pp.

Part 2. 52 Tavistock Square, March 17-29, 1926. 25 pp.

Part 3. April 30, 1926 - September 15 [1926]. 193 pp.

"The Voyage Out."
    Early typescript with author's corrections. Incomplete. Undated. 320 pp.
    Chapters 15-27. Holograph draft. Dated 38 Brunswick Square, March 29,
      1912, and Clifford's Inn, December 21, 1912. 2 vols.
    Later typescript with author's corrections. 407 pp.
    Fragment. 8 pp. Marked "Odd pages" by Leonard Woolf.
    Final typescript fragment with author's corrections. 37 pp.
    Chapters 14, 20, 23, 26, and 27. Holograph and typewritten fragments.

Additional references

Annan, Noel Gilroy. *Leslie Stephen: His Thought and Character in Relation to His Time.* Cambridge, Massachusetts: Harvard University Press, 1952.

Auerbach, Erich. *Mimesis.* Princeton: Princeton University Press, 1953.

Bazin, Nancy Topping. "Virginia Woolf's Quest for Equilibrium." *Modern Language Quarterly,* vol. 32, no. 3 (September 1971), pp. 305-319.

Beach, Joseph Warren. *The Twentieth Century Novel: Studies in Technique.* New York and London: Appleton Century Crofts, 1932.

Beja, Morris. *Epiphany in the Novel.* Seattle: University of Washington Press, 1971.

Bell, Clive. *Art.* London: Chatto and Windus, 1913.

Bell, Clive. *Civilization.* New York; Harcourt, Brace & Co., 1926.

Bell, Clive. *Old Friends, Personal Recollections.* London: Chatto and Windus, 1956.

Bell, Clive. "Virginia Woolf." *Dial* 77 (December 1924):451-465.

Bell, Quentin. *Bloomsbury.* Pageant of History Series. Edited by John Gross. London: George Weidenfeld and Nicolson, 1968.

Bell, Quentin. "The Biographer, the Critic, and the Lighthouse." *Ariel* 2 (January 1971):94-101.

Bell, Quentin. "The Life, Work, and Influence of Roger Fry." Introduction to a catalog for "An exhibition arranged by the Arts Council and the University of Nottingham, 1966."

Bell, Quentin. *Virginia Woolf: A Biography.* 2 vols. London: Hogarth Press, 1972-1973.

Bennett, Joan. *Virginia Woolf: Her Art as a Novelist.* New York: Harcourt, Brace & Co., 1945.

Blackstone, Bernard. *Virginia Woolf: A Commentary.* London: Hogarth Press, 1949.

Blotner, Joseph. "Mythic Patterns in *To the Lighthouse.*" *PMLA* 71 (September 1956):547-562.

Brewster, Dorothy. *Virginia Woolf.* New York: New York University Press, 1962.

Brown, E. K. *Rhythm in the Novel.* Toronto: University of Toronto Press, 1950.

Brown, Robert Curtis. "Laurence Sterne and Virginia Woolf." *University of Kansas City Review* 26 (Autumn 1959):153-159.

Chambers, R. L. *The Novels of Virginia Woolf.* Edinburgh and London: Olivier & Boyd, 1947.

Clutton-Brook, Alan. "Vanessa Bell and Her Circle." *The Listener,* May 4, 1961, pp. 790-791.

Cornwell, Ethel F. *The Still Point: Themes and Variations in the Writings of T. S. Eliot, Coleridge, Yeats, Henry James, Virginia Woolf and D. H. Lawrence.* New Brunswick, N. J.: Rutgers University Press, 1962.

Daiches, David. *The Novel and the Modern World.* Phoenix Books, rev. ed. Chicago: University of Chicago Press, 1960.

Daiches, David. *Virginia Woolf.* Norfolk: New Directions, 1942.

Derbyshire, S. H. "An Analysis of Mrs. Woolf's *To the Lighthouse.*" *College English* 3 (1942):353-360.

Dolle, Erika. *Experiment und Tradition in der Prosa Virginia Woolfs.* Munich: Wilhelm Fink, 1971.

Doner, Dean. "Virginia Woolf: The Service of Style." *Modern Fiction Studies* 2 (February 1956):1-12.

Edel, Leon. *The Modern Psychological Novel.* New York: Grosset and Dunlap, 1964.

Eliot, T. S. "Virginia Woolf." *Horizon* 3 (May 1941):313-316.

Ellmann, Richard. "Two Faces of Edward." *Edwardians and Late Victorians: English Institute Essays. 1959.* Edited with a foreword by Richard Ellmann. New York: Columbia University Press, 1960.

Fleischman, Avrom. *The English Historical Novel: Walter Scott to Virginia Woolf.* Baltimore and London: Johns Hopkins Press, 1971.

Forster, E. M. *Aspects of the Novel.* New York: Harcourt, Brace and World, 1927.

Forster, E. M. "The Early Novels of Virginia Woolf." *Abinger Harvest.* London: Edward Arnold, 1925.

Forster, E. M. *Virginia Woolf: The Rede Lecture, 1941.* New York: Harcourt, Brace and Co., 1942.

Freedman, Ralph. *The Lyrical Novel: Studies in Herman Hesse, Andre Gide, and Virginia Woolf.* Princeton: Princeton University Press, 1963.

Friedman, Melvin. *Stream of Consciousness: A Study in Literary Method.* New Haven: Yale University Press, 1955.

Fry, Roger. *The Artist and Psychoanalysis.* London: Hogarth Press, 1924.

Fry, Roger. *Letters of Roger Fry.* 2 vols. Edited by Denys Sutton. London: Chatto and Windus, 1972.

Fry, Roger. "Sensibility." *Last Lectures.* New York: The Macmillan Co., 1939.

Fry, Roger. *Transformations: Critical and Speculative Essays on Art.* New York: Doubleday Anchor Books, 1956.

Fry, Roger. *Vision and Design.* New York: The World Publishing Co., 1920.

Graham, J. W. "Point of View in *The Waves:* Some Services of the Style." *University of Toronto Quarterly* 29 (April 1970):193-211.

Grant, Duncan. "Virginia Woolf." *Horizon* 3 (June 1941):402-406.

Guiguet, Jean. *Virginia Woolf and Her Works.* Translated from the French by Jean Stewart. London: The Hogarth Press, 1965.

Hafley, James. *The Glass Roof*. Berkeley: University of California Press, 1954.

Hampshire, Stuart N. *Modern Writers and Other Essays*. London: Chatto and Windus, 1970.

Heilbrun, Carolyn. *Toward a Recognition of Androgyny*. New York: Alfred A. Knopf, 1972.

Hoffman, Charles G. "From Short Story to Novel: The Manuscript Revisions of Virginia Woolf's *Mrs. Dalloway*." *Modern Fiction Studies*, vol. 14, no. 2 (Summer, 1968):171-186.

Holtby, Winifred. *Virginia Woolf*. London: Wishart, 1932.

Hulcoop, John F. "Virginia Woolf's Diaries: Some Reflections after Reading Them and a Censure of Mr. Holroyd." *Bulletin of the New York Public Library*, 75 (September 1971):301-310.

Humphrey, Robert. *Stream of Consciousness in the Modern Novel: A Study of James Joyce, Virginia Woolf, Dorothy Richardson, William Faulkner and Others*. Berkeley and Los Angeles: University of California Press, 1959.

Johnstone, J. K. *The Bloomsbury Group: A Study of E. M. Forster, Lytton Strachey, Virginia Woolf, and Their Circle*. New York: Noonday Press, 1954.

Kirkpatrick, B. J. *A Bibliography of Virginia Woolf*. London: Rupert Hart-Davis, 1957.

Kronenberger, Louis. "Virginia Woolf as Critic." *The Republic of Letters: Essays on Various Writers*. New York: Knopf, 1955.

Kumar, Shiv. K. *Bergson and the Stream of Consciousness Novel*. New York: New York University Press, 1962.

Latham, Jacqueline E. M., editor. *Critics on Virginia Woolf: Readings in Literary Criticism*. Miami: University of Miami Press, 1970.

Latham, Jacqueline E. M. "The Model for Clarissa Dalloway–Kitty Maxse." *Notes and Queries* 26:262-263.

Leaska, Mitchell. *Virginia Woolf's Lighthouse: A Study in Critical Method*. New York: Columbia University Press, 1970.

Lehmann, John. "Working with Virginia Woolf." *The Listener*, January 15, 1955, pp. 60-62.

Lester, John A., Jr. *Journey Through Despair: 1880-1914*. Princeton: Princeton University Press, 1968.

Lewis, Wyndham. *Men Without Art*. London: Cassell, 1934.

Love, Jean O. *Worlds in Consciousness: Mythopoetic Thought in the Novels of Virginia Woolf*. Berkeley, Los Angeles, and London: University of California Press, 1970.

Macaulay, Rose. "Virginia Woolf." *Horizon* 3 (May 1941):316-318.

Maitland, Frederic William. *The Life and Letters of Leslie Stephen*. New York: G. P. Putnam's Sons, 1906.

Marder, Herbert. *Feminism and Art: A Study of Virginia Woolf*. Chicago: University of Chicago Press, 1968.

Miller, J. Hillis. "Virginia Woolf's All Soul's Day: The Omniscient Narrator in *Mrs. Dalloway*." *The Shaken Realist: Essays in Modern Literature in Honor of Frederick J. Hoffman*. Baton Rouge: Louisiana State University Press, 1970.

Moody, A. D. *Virginia Woolf.* Edinburgh: Olivier & Boyd, 1963.

Newton, Deborah. *Virginia Woolf.* Melbourne, Australia: University Press, 1946.

Plomer, William. "Virginia Woolf." *Horizon* 3 (May 1941):323-327.

Proudfit, Sharon Wood. "Lily Briscoe's Painting: A Key to Personal Relations in *To the Lighthouse.*" *PMLA* 58 (December 1958): 585-600.

Rachman, Shalom. "Clarissa's Attic: Virginia Woolf's *Mrs. Dalloway* Reconsidered." *Twentieth Century Literature* 58 (January 1972):3-19.

Rantavaara, Irma. *Virginia Woolf and Bloomsbury.* Helsinki: Suomaleisen Tiedeakemien Toimituksia, Annales Academiae Fennicae, 1953.

Richter, Hervena. *Virginia Woolf: The Inward Voyage.* Princeton: The Princeton University Press, 1970.

Rosenbaum, S. P. "The Philosophical Realism of Virginia Woolf." *English Literature and British Philosophy.* Ed. by S. P. Rosenbaum. Chicago: University of Chicago Press, 1971.

Sackville-West, Vita. "Virginia Woolf." *Horizon* 3 (May 1941):318-323.

Schaefer, Josephine O'Brien. *The Three-Fold Nature of Reality.* The Hague: Mouton, 1965.

Schorer, Mark. "Virginia Woolf." *The Yale Review* 30 (December 1942): 379.

Sprague, Claire, ed. *Virginia Woolf: A Collection of Critical Essays.* Englewood Cliffs, N.J.: Prentice-Hall, 1971.

Steinmann, Theodore. "Virginia Woolf: *To the Lighthouse:* die doppelt Funktion der Malerin." *Neuen Sprachen,* vol. 19, no. 11 (November 1970), pp. 537-547.

Thakur, N. C. *The Symbolism of Virginia Woolf.* London: Oxford University Press, 1965.

Troy, William. "Virginia Woolf and the Novel of Sensibility." *Selected Essays.* New Brunswick, N.J.: Rutgers University Press, 1967.

Woolf, Leonard. *Beginning Again: An Autobiography of the Years* 1911-1918. New York: Harcourt, Brace and World, 1963.

Woolf, Leonard. *Growing: An Autobiography of the Years 1904-1911.* New York: Harcourt, Brace and Co., 1962.

Woolf, Leonard. *Sowing: An Autobiography of the Years 1880-1904.* New York: Harcourt, Brace and World, 1960.

Woolf, Leonard. *The Journey not the Arrival Matters: An Autobiography of the Years 1939-1969.* New York: Harcourt, Brace and World, 1969.

Index

The razor edge
of balance

Virginia Woolf's search for balance, a clear-cut and consistent process from her early childhood fiction to her last novel, is the core of this enlightening and sensitive critical study.

In making the literary break from the Edwardian school of Galsworthy, Wells, and Bennett, Virginia Woolf was a highly conscious writer with a very clear concept of what she was attempting to do.

Part 1 of this work examines Woolf's theories of fictional form, criticism, and aesthetics through her own reviews of contemporary fiction and through her comments on her own methods of composition. Her early novels are analyzed in Part 2, which describes how Woolf worked out these theories and how they are most successfully embodied in *To the Lighthouse*. While Woolf has been conceived by some as a gloomy, dark, and serious writer, Jane Novak reveals the wit and humor, the urbanity and nuances in her personality.

Described as "fair and clear and perceptive . . . not, like some other Woolfian criticism, sentimental or gushing or abstruse," *The Razor Edge of Balance* reflects the wealth of material now available in recently released primary sources. To enrich her study Dr. Novak has delved into memorabilia, correspondence, reading notes, diaries, notebooks, and unpublished manuscripts in the Berg Collection at the New York Public Library, the British Museum, the Charleston Papers, the Monks House Papers, and the Papers of E. M. Forster. Some extracts from private letters are published here for the first time.